BUILDING THE FAITH COMMUNITY

BUILDING THE FAITH COMMUNITY

by
Cora Marie Dubitsky

PAULIST PRESS
New York / Paramus / Toronto

Copyright © 1974 by
The Missionary Society
of St. Paul the Apostle
in the State of New York

All rights reserved. No part of this book may be reproduced or transmitted in any form or by any means, electronic or mechanical, including photocopying, recording or by any information storage and retrieval system, without permission in writing from the Publisher.

Library of Congress
Catalog Card Number: 74-12632

ISBN: 0-8091-1848-3

Published by Paulist Press
Editorial Office: 1865 Broadway, N.Y., N.Y. 10023
Business Office: 400 Sette Drive, Paramus, N.J. 07652

Printed and bound in the
United States of America

CONTENTS

Preface 1

PART ONE
THE PROCESS OF EDUCATION

1. Religious Education 9

2. Education and Developmental Psychology 22

3. Philosophy and the Meaning of
   Human Existence 33

4. Belief and Faith 44

PART TWO
MESSAGE

5. Revelation and Truth 61

6. Trinity and Creation 75

7. Sin and Evil 95

PART THREE
COMMUNITY

8. Worship and Prayer 111

9. The Sacramental Life 131

PART FOUR
SERVICE

10. The Moral Life 145

11. The Kingdom and the Future 162

To the Dubitsky Family

REFERENCES

TT	To Teach As Jesus Did
GCD	General Catechetical Directory
RE/BT	Religious Education / Basic Teachings

Vatican II Documents

AA	Decree on the Apostolate of the Laity
AG	Decree on the Missionary Activity of the Church
CD	Decree on the Bishops' Pastoral Office in the Church
DH	Declaration on Religious Freedom
DV	Dogmatic Constitution on Divine Revelation
GE	Declaration on Religious Education
GS	Pastoral Constitution on the Church in the Modern World
LG	Dogmatic Constitution on the Church
OT	Decree on Priestly Formation

Preface

During Vatican Council II, the bishops of the Catholic Church agreed that Catholic teaching must confront current realities and be presented "in a manner adapted to the needs of the time." They called attention to the ongoing need for dialogue with the wider human community in which Catholics live. Furthermore, they declared, the message that Catholics proclaim must be "distinguished by clarity of speech."

In order to meet this challenge, help unify our efforts, and enable us to clarify our position, the Church, since 1971, has endorsed the publication of three documents dealing with religious education: *The General Catechetical Directory, To Teach As Jesus Did*, and *Religious Education/The Basic Teachings*. If all catechists were "thoroughly acquainted" with the doctrine of the Church and had adequate knowledge of psychological principles as called for by the bishops in council, these documents could be adequate guides. However, many religion teachers are volunteers who have not had an opportunity to develop the rich professional background they know they should have. Many feel incapable of implementing adequately the directives of the bishops.

It is for these volunteer religion teachers that this book is written. It is for teachers who are unaccustomed to reading documents written in technical or "churchy" language. It is for teachers who may have only an intuitional grasp of some of the basic religious concepts such as faith, grace, sacrament.

Questions generally posed by volunteer religion teachers suggest three major concerns: (1) the need for professional background in religious studies and in related disciplines, (2) the need for assurance that the content of the religion texts they must use represents the authentic teaching of the Church, (3) the need for training in teaching methods and techniques.

The major thrust of this book is directed toward the satisfaction of the first need. Since volunteer religion teachers usually have busy outside schedules, they cannot be expected to spend an excessive amount of time traveling to distant centers to take courses in content or methods. Therefore, the insights from contemporary studies in psychology, philosophy, and education have been incorporated into this manual for easy reference.

In order to meet the second need, each chapter is followed by a paraphrase of relevant official pronouncements taken from Vatican documents and the three pastoral statements on religious education mentioned above. Specific references are included to facilitate individual research and to help religious education coordinators develop a systematic study of the documents.

This is not a "how to" manual. Much has already been written about teaching methods and techniques. Yet no technique is ultimately successful unless the teacher understands both the material and the student. As the bishops point out: "No method frees the catechist from the personal task of assimilating the material and passing judgment on concrete cases" (GCD

71). Teachers who have an adequate grasp of basic concepts and can relate them to a total picture are in a better position to translate these concepts into the thought patterns of the child. The teacher with a narrow perspective must cling to the teacher's manual and can only repeat the words of some "authority." Such a teacher is easily threatened by questions that are not anticipated. It is hoped that this book will enhance his self-confidence and sense of security by widening his horizons.

While this book can be used by the individual teacher as a reference tool, it is suggested that it might prove more valuable if used as an in-service teaching guide. The plan followed in Holy Name Parish in Bloomfield, Indiana, is outlined here to suggest a feasible alternative for those parishes that experience difficulty in setting up any kind of a training program for their volunteer religion teachers. A major portion of the material in this book was discussed with the teachers of Holy Name Parish during our in-service sessions.

First, the opening of religious education classes was postponed one month so that each Sunday morning, during the hour when the volunteers would have been scheduled to teach, the teachers might participate in the educational program designed to improve their professional status. One Sunday each month is set aside as teacher-education day. On this Sunday, there is a general program for all the students which, in our case, is handled by the coordinator. This frees the teachers for an extra hour of continuing education each month. The plan is especially desirable because it makes no excessive demands upon the teacher. The teachers are expected to devote to these activities only the number of hours already volunteered.

In order to acquaint the teachers with available teaching aids, audiovisual materials, and the services of the diocesan staff, a special full-day program was planned. A priest with experience in the field of religious education spoke on issues raised by the teachers and celebrated the special liturgy planned by the teachers. Representatives from the diocesan office of education brought samples of available materials and described their services. Films were viewed, and their potential for classroom use was explored in group discussion. This arrangement does not, of course, exhaust the possibilities. Hopefully, it will serve as a springboard for innovative planning for the continuing education of volunteer religion teachers in other parishes.

If this book is to be used as a guide for the continuing education of religion teachers, perhaps it would be beneficial for teachers to read each chapter before the training session. If the content raises any problems or questions, teachers should be encouraged to write down their questions as precisely as possible. These can then be discussed among coordinators and staff members in a communal effort to arrive at a deeper understanding of fundamental issues.

Another reason for having teachers read the material beforehand is that, if the content has already been assimilated, the work sessions might be used for the application of theory to practice. For example, after having read the first chapter, teachers might want to spend some time alone or in groups formulating the major goals and the task objectives for specific lessons. Some time might be spent in examining the curriculum to see how well the religious education program integrates message, community, and service.

The book is divided into four parts. Part One

presents the conceptual framework for the interpretation of the ideas presented in later chapters. This introductory section is indispensable in the understanding of novel approaches to traditional themes. Although the later chapters may be read in any sequential order, it is suggested that they not be read before those in Part One so the reader can make the most effective use of each presentation.

Parts Two, Three, and Four are an attempt to present an integrated view of different dimensions of religious belief and practice. The questions the writer asked herself before beginning any chapter were: "How can this subject shed light on the meaning of human existence as we experience it from day to day? What do we do in everyday life that is carried over into the practice of our religion?" It is hoped that these reflections will bring fresh vitality to those religious beliefs and practices that have become routine or which we take for granted.

In many ways, the preparation of this manuscript has been a community project. I am grateful to Mary Anne Farris, who suggested that I try to publish the material I was then sharing with the teachers at Holy Name Parish in Bloomfield, Indiana. My thanks go to: the religion teachers at Holy Name for their positive response and active participation in the discussion of the contents of this book; Father Smith, pastor, for his openness and cooperation; Wendy Allen who, in spite of other pressures, managed a superb typing job; Jan Miracle for proofreading the draft; Sister Eunice North and Sister Mildred Kane for their continued prayers and support; Father Bob Borchertmeyer for reading the manuscript and sharing invaluable insights, criticisms, and suggestions.

PART ONE

THE PROCESS OF EDUCATION

The process of education understood in its broadest philosophic sense is a continuing search for the meaning and purpose of individual and communal existence. By removing the threat of meaninglessness, education offers us an opportunity for genuine happiness. Socialization through education is an important element in developing our capacity for human imagination. Imagination enables us to comprehend what it means to be another person while, at the same time, affirming our own humanity. We cannot reach out in genuine care and concern until we can picture ourselves in the place of another. Generosity, which education should engender, is the capacity to participate imaginatively in the experiences of ot' persons and communities and to direct our to their well-being without calculation of

1. Religious Education

If we are to be effective as religious educators, we must have a clear idea of what we are trying to achieve. We cannot talk about religious education unless we first clarify our notion of education itself. As we examine more closely the meaning of education and the purpose of education, we shall begin to grasp, among other things, the significance of the recent change in our terminology from "religious instruction" to "religious education."

In general, education is a society's way of transmitting its values and culture. Education is a way of helping individuals form appropriate dispositions toward nature, their fellowmen, and themselves. Since our very being is part of a larger world, our fulfillment depends on the degree to which we achieve dispositions of care and concern for this world. The educated man is one who has grasped the simple fact that to be a person is to be related to the human and non-human beings in the world. Education is a teaching-learning process which enables a person to widen the scope of these relationships and to develop an ever-expanding picture of the whole.

Education is not the mere acquisition of data or bits and fragments of information. While knowledge implies a systematic grasp of principles and a perception of logical relationships among facts and concepts, education is not even limited to knowledge. Genuine education must lead eventually to wisdom. Through the centuries, the wise man has been characterized by a magnanimous spirit. His unifying vision of human existence gives his life a wholeness, a kind of integrity. One who is wise applies his learning and knowledge to the enrichment of his daily activities.

In one of his poems T.S. Eliot asks: "Where is the knowledge we lost in information? Where is the wisdom we lost in knowledge?" Unless we direct our educational efforts to the attainment of wisdom, we may end up asking the question that Eliot eventually raises: "Where is the life we lost in living?"

Religious education, then, is a commonly accepted way of transmitting our Christian heritage. Its purpose is the development of those dispositions toward ourselves, our fellowman, the world, and God which can properly be called "Christian." Religious education provides an individual with the opportunity to learn how to "put on Christ"; to assume his attitudes, to accept his value-system, and to acquire his vision.

Authentic teaching is an essential component of education. Teaching is an intentional attempt to bring about in a learner some kind of understanding coupled with a disposition to use that understanding in appropriate ways. Authentic teaching is an attempt to reach the whole person: reason, will, and emotion. Genuine teaching has a restricted range which can more easily be grasped by looking at a "teaching continuum" designed by an educational philosopher:

Behavior, Conduct				*Knowledge, Beliefs*
Intimidation	Training	Authentic Teaching	Instructing	Propagandizing
Threatening	Conditioning	Dialogue	Indoctrinating	Lying

REGION OF INTELLIGENCE

Notice that training and instructing are on the borderline of authentic teaching. This does not mean that training and instructing are inauthentic ways of imparting information. It does point out, though, that these two modes are not strictly synonymous with authentic teaching. In other words, teaching is more than training, which relies heavily on conditioning; it is more than instructing which relies, in large part, on indoctrination. Instruction has connotations of technical procedures or laws to be followed. Training implies the acquisition of habitual modes of behavior through repetitive activity.

Social psychologists talk about the socialization process that occurs in all organizations. They tell us that the effectiveness of an organization depends on its ability to socialize new members. This is the process by which the individual acquires the norms, values, attitudes, and behavioral responses that characterize the group to which he hopes to belong. It includes those learnings that are the "price of membership." Inevitably, the process includes some indoctrination and training in what the organization feels is important. However, the success of the organization will depend on how well it can take the individual beyond this initiation to a point of personal commitment and loyalty.

Propagandizing and intimidation, of course, have no place in religious education. The Church has come to acknowledge the futility of force in spreading the Gospel. To win compliance through a threat of eternal damnation is the least effective way to develop personal commitment and growth in faith. Propaganda is more easily overlooked. Yet, this is what takes place when a teacher uses such slogans as "the Church says" to back up a personal stance that is difficult to defend on rational grounds. Teachers ought to be aware of the fact that the Scriptures can be invoked to support almost any political position or ideology. When the Bible is used as this kind of weapon, a subtle form of deception is taking place.

Teaching implies unfinished inquiry into the meaning of the subject matter. The unfinished nature of inquiry means that at no stage are our beliefs "unshakable" in the sense that they cannot be improved upon. In principle, they are subject to expansion, revision, and even contradiction. Our beliefs, however, are not whimsical or arbitrary, and it would be absurd to think that a person might change his fundamental principles every other day. When students are brought to an awareness of the contingent character of human knowledge, they are better prepared to continue developing the concepts to which they have been introduced.

Much of the confusion in the Church at present stems from our absolutizing tendencies in the past. Attempts at renewal are often frustrated by adults who were indoctrinated to believe that the information they received as children was totally adequate for any future exigency. In many cases, their instruction was perceived to be both complete and unchangeable. Frequently, these same adults are too inflexible to accept the fact of change in the Church and feel too threatened even to inquire into the rationale for the change. Some prefer to remain aloof; others go the other route by rejecting Church teaching.

Learning is a process involving various types of behavior: thinking, doing, feeling, willing. It involves a sequence of events and outcomes. Learning depends upon what the learner does—how he perceives, how he thinks, how he feels, and how he acts. The learner must in some way act upon or react to the situation he encounters. There can be no learning unless he responds in some way.

Since learning depends upon what the learner does, activating the class becomes crucial in achieving the objective of the lesson. The teacher must create learning situations that will stimulate the student to listen, to read, to write, to discuss, to ask questions, to perform tasks, to solve problems, to make things, to think critically, or to engage in other activities that might be appropriate to the expected learning outcome.

Teaching is an intentional activity; it is not random busyness. Often, a teacher decides how much material will be covered and assumes that the students will learn without ever thinking through what is meant by "learning the material." In other words, the teacher fails to formulate the objectives of the teaching-learning process. Yet, there is no way to evaluate our religion classes or to improve their quality unless we, as teachers, know what we first set out to accomplish.

One of the trends in education today is to focus on evaluation as an essential ingredient in every lesson plan. Evaluation is a measure of the difference between what we intend to do and what actually happens. What we intend to do is called our objective or goal. It is the reason why we initiate any activity. Ordinarily, a series of different activities takes place during a class period. Each activity is designed to move the class closer to the main goal. The aim of each activity is called a task objective. Each objective is a stepping-stone to the final goal. These objectives can be classified as cognitive, affective, or active.

A cognitive outcome might be to know more, to have more information, to develop concepts that are new to the students, to recognize things not previously known, to increase the complexity of understanding, to understand more implications, to think more critically or analytically. Affective outcomes deal with ways the teacher wants the student to feel toward the values presented, the kind of emotional reaction desired, motivational trends, attitudes, and appreciations. Active outcomes have to do with observable or productive behavior. It must be remembered that such directly observable activity does not necessarily indicate understanding or appreciation. Whether the objectives of a lesson are actually achieved depends, to a great extent, on the teacher's awareness of such relationships while planning and carrying out the teaching activity.

So far, we have seen that lesson planning involves three distinct tasks: the identification of the major goal, the formation of intermediate task objectives, and evaluation. Evaluation is particularly helpful in locating strengths and weaknesses in presentation. When a teacher notices that what is intended is not what takes place in the classroom, she is alerted to the problem areas. The goal and objectives, however, will be of little use unless they are specific, realistic, and attainable. They cannot remain in the mind; they must be written. Writing them down helps us to clarify our ideas.

In order to assist teachers in writing their goals, the following goal-analysis procedure is offered. Suppose it is stated that the goal of a particular lesson is "to be a better Christian." What signs would we have at the end of the class period that our students are better Christians? Is this goal attainable in the time allotted? Secondly, there are innumerable ways to become better Christians. Which way is being emphasized? Is the goal specific? During a class period, can we transform our students into better Christians? Is the goal realistic? While this goal is certainly a noble one, it is a decision that the student makes in response to Christ. The teacher can only provide an atmosphere in which such a decision is made easier or more attractive.

Now let us turn our attention to a goal that seems more concrete: "to learn the ten commandments." Does this mean that we want the students to be able to recite the ten commandments or to understand the meaning of each one? The goal needs clarification. If we are concerned with understanding, the goal cannot be attained in one lesson. Each lesson aims at a short-range goal which serves the long-range goal of the entire program. In this case, "to learn the ten commandments" should be considered a long-range goal.

Formulating appropriate goals is not difficult but it does require some practice. The extra effort, however, can have certain desirable effects. Making goals more explicit helps teachers discern the essential elements in a lesson plan. This, in turn, can free them from over-dependence upon the teachers' manual. When they feel they have a "hold" on the material, their self-confidence is enhanced. Teachers who are comfortable with the content can be more creative with its utilization. Just because a lesson has been "covered" does not mean the objectives of the lesson have been met.

Where do the intermediate task objectives belong? Perhaps, if we work through a lesson plan, all the elements will fall into place. Let us say that our theme is prayer. As we read through the teachers' guide, we notice that the lesson is not about prayer in general but rather about prayer in the life of a Christian. Our lesson plan might look somewhat like the following:

GOAL: to become more aware of the place of prayer in the life of a Christian. (Remember, the goal tells us the reason why we are teaching this lesson.)

INTERMEDIATE TASK OBJECTIVES (Goal Oriented Activities):

1. to explore some Gospel accounts of Jesus at prayer,
2. to discuss the place of prayer in our lives as followers of Jesus,
3. to share an experience of prayer.

Evaluation of the success of each activity gives the teacher some indication of the degree to which the main goal was realized. Whether the students actually become more prayerful is beyond the scope of the lesson. However, their awareness of the place of prayer in the lives of Christians can be measured to some extent by their class response.

Some religion teachers are opposed to the idea of writing specific, measurable goals. They say, "Faith cannot be measured." While this is true, it misses the point. Evaluation does not aim at measuring faith. It is a way of finding out if, as teachers, we accomplished what we had set out to do. Evaluation helps us keep a proper perspective. It helps us to focus on those things we can control to some extent. We can try to create an environment in which the Word of God can take deeper root. We can pray for the Spirit to speak through us. None of us can assume the power of God who alone calls persons to faith.

Effective teaching is more than the attainment of objectives, however. In teaching, there can be no unfailing recipe for combining the right ingredients to obtain certain, predictable effects because teaching is not

Religious Education

technology. Nevertheless, any teacher can improve if helped to analyze performance in the light of existing knowledge about the teaching-learning process.

Teacher personality, for example, is a variable that affects the nature of the interaction that takes place in the classroom. A personality trait that colors the entire teaching activity is the teacher's tolerance for ambiguity. Teachers with high tolerance levels are comfortable in unstructured situations and are likely to be flexible or permissive. Those with low tolerance levels need organization and set procedures. Carried to extremes, neither one is desirable. It must be remembered that the students also have different tolerance levels. Some students need more structure and guidance than others. A teacher who can accommodate students' needs for structure while allowing room for creative expression is in a better position to increase student satisfaction.

Sometimes, teachers are concerned about their authority in the classroom and about the amount of control they should exercise. Some fear that any form of discipline stifles initiative and may engender a dislike for religion. In the matter of control, it might be good to remember that, in the final analysis, the only thing the teacher can control is his own behavior. The teacher can control the time and interest he puts into class preparation. The teacher can control the development of his own professional background. In the classroom, the teacher can control his responses and reactions to students. All these activities demand self-discipline. Without discipline, there is no growth in freedom. Without discipline, we merely follow random impulse. Students also need self-discipline. They may have to be reminded that they live in the world with others and that their own fulfillment as persons demands that they be aware of how their behavior affects others.

While the subject of curriculum will not be pursued here, something must be said about the need to be relevant. "Relevant" is an ambiguous term and is often interpreted to mean whatever happens to attract the students' immediate interest. But the attention of students is often captured by current fads. In their search for relevance, teachers sometimes lay aside the content that belongs specifically to religious education and direct their energies to the investigation of the current fad. Such procedure may, in the long run, be almost totally irrelevant. If, after the fad has passed, the student does not have something stable to which he can be committed, the teacher's efforts have been wasted. Of course, the teacher is not dispensed from the responsibility of helping the student to see how new knowledge relates to the student's life. The teacher must be able to communicate to the student how the subject matter in which the student had not previously been interested can enrich the meaning of life and lead to genuine happiness.

There is a fourth component in education that we have not yet considered. Along with teacher, learner, and curriculum, the educational setting has an influence on what will be learned. The setting is more than the room or building. It includes administrators, counselors, and teaching staff. It embraces all the policies and regulations that contribute to the distinctive atmosphere of the educational enterprise. How teachers interact among themselves and with the parish priests communicates to the student something of the significance or unimportance of religious education in that parish.

If religious education aims at building community,

catechists must be more than a group of teachers who perform their functions apart from one another. Social psychologists who have studied organizational effectiveness tell us of the importance of the "corporate image." This concept includes notions about the significance of the group to which one belongs. Belonging to the group inspires enthusiasm and commitment. Volunteer response seems to be greater in parishes where volunteers are publicly acknowledged as being vital to the life of the parish. Some parishes have special ceremonies during the liturgy which focus on the teachers and identify them as the official parish educators. Others use the parish bulletin for public expressions of gratitude. This does not infer that religion teachers seek praise or reward for their efforts. It merely acknowledges the fact that, as human beings, they need the support of the community. To say "we need you" and never follow through with actions that affirm that statement is mere formalism.

Our sense of community must extend beyond the boundaries of the parish. Not too much extra effort is needed to make arrangements with nearby parishes for the sharing of resources and personnel. If the parishes must incur additional expenses to carry on the program for the continuing education of the teachers, it might be wise to combine forces and set up one program from which a few parishes might benefit. Cutting down expenses is a factor that any nonprofit organization must take seriously. But sharing is important for another reason. Parishes are not in a competitive market. To preach personal detachment from material possessions while hesitating as a parish to share our resources with other parishes is to lack credibility.

In summary, religious education is an indispensable means by which the Church carries out her mission. Discourse about education must go beyond teachers and texts to include learning theory, principles of curriculum, and the setting in which learning takes place. In order to increase the effectiveness of religious education in the parish, some type of program for the continuing education of the volunteer religion teacher seems mandatory. Through religious education, we ought to be able to say that we really do "have a reason for the hope that is in us."

DOCUMENTATION

Religious education derives its meaning and function from the mission of the Church. This implies not only that we be aware of the general goals of religious education but also that we see how these goals fit into the context of that mission. It is not surprising, then, that the description of the mission of the Church in the Vatican II documents is similar to the statements about the goals of religious education. (TT 7)

The following chart may help us to see the relationship between the two. If we place alongside the chart the three dimensions of religious education, we can see how the latter follow the pattern of the goals. (TT 14)

CHURCH	RELIGIOUS EDUCATION	DIMENSIONS
to make known the message of the Gospel	to enable the individual to pattern his life on the message of Christ	Message GS 92 TT 8
to bring people together in unity in the Spirit	to form persons-in-community	Community GS 92 GCD 38 TT 11, 13
to spread the Kingdom of God	to bring about social reform	Service AA 2 TT 8, 10

Religious Education

These goals are quite general since they are intended to encompass all aspects of religious education at any age level and in any circumstances. Secondly, these are long-range goals. They represent the ideal toward which we direct our efforts, knowing that we shall never attain it. It is like the horizon that is always before us outlining objects against the sky. This does not infer that we cannot reach goals in religious education. It merely points out that our program and lesson goals must be aimed in the same direction. They must be integrated into a unified whole. (TT 92, 93)

Modern pedagogical methods will not serve the cause of religious education if the content lacks either relevance or orthodoxy. If religious education is to foster unity, cooperative efforts must be made among bishops, pastors, religious educators, and parents. There must be an evaluation of the religious education program in order to determine its effectiveness in transmitting the authentic Christian message. Improved channels of communication among all those responsible for religious education can help in clarifying some of the issues that produce tensions within the Christian community. (TT 53, 54, 55)

The education of religion teachers must be continued during the entire time they serve the community in that capacity. To rely on the central diocesan office for this service is not enough. Parishes must devote special attention to it. Pastors and directors of religious education programs have a duty to see to it that the teachers are given an opportunity for continued learning. The objective of such a formation program is a development of aptitude and the ability to communicate the message of the Gospel. This, in turn, requires formation in theology, the human sciences, and methodology. (GCD 110)

2. Education and Developmental Psychology

Children do not think as adults. Although it might seem obvious to us now, it took adults a long time to realize that a child is not an "homunculus," a little man. A child interprets the world according to his own experience of that world. While adults also interpret the world according to their own experiences, their thought patterns are different. Adults have countless numbers of well-developed concepts from which to draw. The child has fewer concepts, and, because of his lack of experience, many of these are not well formed. The child needs time and experience to develop concepts to go with the words he hears and uses. How much time he needs depends on his intellectual capacity and his opportunities for learning.

Contemporary psychological theory has much to contribute to those who must plan learning opportunities. While this theory can provide us with tools for improving our teaching methods, it does not supply ready-made answers to specific problems. Between the fund of knowledge about human development on one end and the application of that knowledge in the classroom on the other lies the teacher's understanding.

The road from knowledge to application is one that must be traveled by the teacher alone. How this knowledge affects the teacher as a person will affect his actions, responses, and reactions in the classroom. Nevertheless, knowledge of the human developmental processes is a step in the right direction.

In all areas of human development growth is gradual. We do not mature in great leaps and bounds. Developmental psychologists usually identify distinct stages of growth. These stages follow a natural sequence, and an individual must follow this order. He cannot skip a stage to move to a higher level regardless of the pressures a teacher may bring to bear upon him. This is especially true of cognitive development.

The following diagram presents a synoptic view of the positions taken by several developmental and philosophical psychologists.

DIMENSIONS OF HUMAN DEVELOPMENT

Stages of Cognitive Development	Levels of Meaning	Stages of Moral Development	Ages
1. Intuitive	1. Sensual	1. Pre-moral	2-4
			5-7
2. Concrete logical	2. Objective	2. Legalistic	8-10
			11-12
3. Abstract logical	3. Spiritual	3. Personal	13-15
			16—

The ages included within each stage are the equivalent mental ages rather than the chronological ages. Furthermore, these represent the average age suggested by various psychologists. The division signifies earlier/later phases. Since children do not progress at the same rate, an understanding of all the stages should enable the teacher to cope more effectively with inequality in the classroom.

Cognitive development is the process by which we become aware, understand, and judge. It is not simply growth in the amount of knowledge we acquire. At the intuitive stage, a child's knowledge is perceptual rather than conceptual. This means that he gains his knowledge through direct use of his senses rather than through elaborate mental processes. For example, if daddy is dressed in a Santa Claus suit, he is no longer daddy. Only Santa Claus is perceived. Furthermore, a child at this stage cannot take into account more than one attribute at a time. The startling results of Goldman's research in religious education shocked religion teachers into an awareness of this fact. Old Testament stories used to be a favored form of entertainment in religion classes for the young. The story of Abraham and Isaac was used as an example of faith and obedience. When the children who had heard this story were asked to interpret it in their own words, it was discovered that the children had missed the point completely. What was conveyed to the children was the notion that any God who would ask Abraham to do such a thing must be cruel indeed.

The child in the concrete logical phase can coordinate series of things. He can see part/whole relationships only if these are concrete. Anyone who has tried to teach fractions to children at this stage knows that the child must manipulate concrete objects and cut them into pieces. Only after much practice in forming wholes out of parts does the child grasp the concept, fraction. The child at this developmental stage can follow directions in putting things together and placing things in categories if he is guided by something he can see, whether it be the written word or concrete object. This way of thinking will be seen more clearly when we discuss the second stage of moral development.

Once the student has arrived at the level of abstract thinking, he can follow the logic of statements of belief, opinion, and doubt. No matter how theoretical the topic, the student can reason from hypotheses to logical conclusions. He can even think about thoughts. Of course, this does not mean that as soon as the student can begin to think abstractly he has mastered all the elements. The teacher, many times, will have to point out relationships that the student has failed to recognize in his analysis of situations or interpretation of events.

Knowledge of the way our thought patterns are formed should help us to understand better the phases of human moral development. Between the ages of two and four, the conscience is not yet formed even though the child has learned to speak. Sometimes, parents confuse the development of the will with the development of conscience. When the child begins to exercise his will by saying "No!" to everything, he is thought to be disobedient. Actually, he is just exercising a newly discovered power and testing it out to see how far it can take him. For a child at this age, words that attract attention have a magical quality.

A Swiss psychologist, Jean Piaget, conducted a series of experiments which revealed the way children interpret rules and the binding power of those rules. Attitudes toward rules and laws help reveal the level of moral development. An essential ingredient in morality is the willingness to accept and follow a system of rules which regulate our interpersonal behavior. These rules can be external or internal. Piaget, of course, worked with external rules so that he could measure the effects in some way. What follows is a summary of some of his findings.

The child at the pre-moral stage *thinks* he is obeying rules when, in fact, he neither understands them nor follows them. For example, in a game of marbles, each of two children will play the game according to his own rules, yet they both think they have followed common rules. Winning the game, therefore, means simply having a good time. The pre-moral child believes that some significant authority established the rules and that no one ever played the game before those rules were established. Once established, the rules are sacred and absolute. They can never be changed. They judge badness by its bigness, not by its motive. The child who spills a glass of milk on the floor to get even with mother is judged to be less blameworthy than the child who accidentally spills a whole quart.

At nine or ten, approximately, a child enters the first phase of the legalistic stage of development. The child can now adhere to an agreed-upon framework even though he is not capable of mastering all the rules. He still experiences conflict and difficulty with the rules. The child at this stage does realize, though, that rules have a social character and have binding power only as long as people are willing to abide by them. He can also see that human beings make the rules and human beings can change them.

By the time the child is eleven or twelve, he can master the rules and exhibit genuine cooperation in a rule-keeping activity. Usually, children in this latter phase display a legalistic fascination with rules. They enjoy settling differences of opinion concerning rules and elaborating upon them. Often, children in this pre-adolescent stage form special clubs and spend a large portion of club-meeting time establishing rules for club leaders and subordinate members. Frequently the clubs go out of existence once the rules have been formulated.

The stage is marked by an "eye for an eye" mentality. Justice means giving the other guy the same raw deal that he gave you. The child at this level still finds it difficult to associate intention with the moral act. He tends to judge actions by concrete results. An example from my own experience can serve as an illustration. While conducting a demonstration class with fifth and sixth graders, I asked them to assume the role of judge in two court cases. The first case involved a man who, while driving home from a party at which he had been drinking, accidentally killed a pedestrian. The second case was that of a man who had worked out a plan to murder someone. His attempt failed, and he was brought into court on charges of attempted murder. The students judged the first case very harshly; yet, they saw no reason for condemning the second. Only after a series of questions and reconsideration of the cases did a sixth grader perceive that personal intention is a significant factor in human relations.

During adolescence, an individual may begin to experience beliefs that seem to contradict those he has been taught. This leads him to reexamine the rules to which he had been giving unquestioning compliance. He is now at the stage where he is capable of taking the first faltering steps in the structuring of a personal value system. He no longer accepts external rules indiscriminately. As he places those rules under closer scrutiny, he may reject some while electing to follow others that he understands and accepts.

Now let us consider the "levels of meaning." Notice that each level corresponds with a stage of cognitive or moral development. A child on the sensual or objective level cannot understand reality on a spiritual level. This does not mean that the child does not intuit or perceive something of the significance of the spiritual. Rather, it indicates that the child's spiritual world often resembles a magical fairyland.

Level of meaning identifies a person's value system. While the adult experiences life on all three levels, he must decide which level will assume the greatest significance for him. The level on which he lives his life most intensely will affect most of his major moral decisions and color his personal relationships. The level on which he interprets his own experiences determines the value he places on persons, events, and things.

The sensual man interprets relationships and activity in terms of the pleasure/pain principle. What makes him "feel good" is good. Pain must be avoided at all costs. Sexual intimacy is good because it is pleasurable. When the pleasure goes, the partner goes. Not too many years ago, some priests ascertained the seriousness of a violation of chastity by the amount of pleasure it afforded the offender! Marriage was valid if it was consummated. The sensual man does not see any reason for going to church because he does not "get anything out of it." In other words, he does not feel exhilarated at Mass. Many of us remember also the arguments over how many minutes Christ remained in the host after it was consumed—Jesus' presence was determined by bodily metabolism!

The individual on the objective level lives in a world of things, quantifiable and measurable. He judges his own stature by the number of things he has acquired. Persons are objects to be manipulated for personal gain. Even in "love" the other person is a possession over which the objective man feels he must have some control. He measures his manhood by the number of his "loves." His love is calculating. If he does something for you, you must do something equivalent for him. If he gives you something, you must reciprocate with a gift of equal value. Laws are external things to which he gives external compliance. "Goodness" is a matter of staying within the limits of the law. This type of individual wants to know how far he can go without breaching the rule. He worries about improving his technique rather than the substance of his activity.

Even sincere Christians can get bogged down on this level and remain impoverished throughout adulthood. Religion is another world of things. A sacrament is a thing that gives us another thing, grace. In fact, grace is an amazing thing having liquid properties. Even if we have some of it, God can pour more of it into us. Even truth is a thing. Since the Catholic Church possesses this truth, it is difficult to understand how other religions can possess the same "thing."

The word spirit refers to the dynamic, humanizing force within each person. A person on the spiritual level, then, interprets his world of relationships within the framework of an interiorized set of values to which he is committed. For him, people are more important than things. Like THE LITTLE PRINCE, he senses that "what is essential is invisible to the naked eye." He is an integrated person whose mind, heart, and body work in harmony. He is a whole person. And as more than one theologian would remind us, "Holiness is wholeness."

The Old Testament has an interesting story about God's efforts to lead a man from the objective to the spiritual level. The man's name was Jonah—as in whale. It seems that Jonah was very much displeased with God for not having destroyed the Ninevites. He hated to see his own prophecy remain unrealized. Yet, when a gourd plant that had been providing shade and comfort for Jonah wilted and died, it was more than he could take. He decided that even death was better than a life without his beloved vine. God then very patiently tried to make Jonah understand life's most important lesson: people are more important than things. Jonah was very much like the 20th century man whose bumper sticker reads: "We need oil, not Jews."

If we glance back at the chart on page 23, we can see that it is possible for adults to have advanced to the third stage of cognitive development without having developed beyond the second stage in moral development. More pathetic is the adult who has hardly advanced beyond the first level of meaning. He is forever deprived of the joy of genuine human relationships. His life is hectic because he is incessantly searching for the happiness that always lies beyond his grasp.

In this chapter, we have seen that learning to think, discern, discriminate, and judge is a slow process. As we develop intellectually and morally, we pass through certain stages marked by rather universal characteristics. When we have achieved the highest level, we do not remain there every moment. It is possible to live on various levels simultaneously. The important task for the individual is that of balanced integration.

DOCUMENTATION

During Vatican Council II, the bishops acknowledged the benefits that can be derived from a knowledge of the secular sciences. They pointed out that advances in psychology and the social sciences can help us to progress to deeper levels of self-knowledge. Modern psychological research enables us to explain human activity more profoundly. The methods of these sciences can help the teacher exert a more direct influence on a group of students. With the help of educational psychology and modern learning theory, teachers can help children and young people in a harmonious development of their physical, moral, and intellectual endowments. Pastors and teachers engaged in religious education are exhorted to use not only theological principles but also findings of psychology and the social sciences. Knowledge from these fields can help all of us to live the life of faith on a more mature level. (GS 5, 54; GE 1; GCD 112, 113)

While catechists are not expected to become expert psychologists, they ought to be made aware of enough of the findings of modern psychological research to be able to choose whatever can help them communicate more easily with their students. Catechists must be able to interpret the reactions and responses of individual students and classes of pupils. Only in this way can they discern the spiritual capacities of the learners. (GCD 112, 113)

Since catechists are expected to use the most effective methodology in teaching, they must give due consideration to the listener's level of maturity and understanding. The method must be appropriate to both the subject matter and the natural disposition, ability, age, and circumstances in life of the learner. Since learning is sequential, teachers should be aware of the proper sequence. Furthermore, the religious truth must be made relevant. This means that it must be presented in such a way that it gives the student a vital or living experience of faith. One can be orthodox and relevant at the same time. (CD 14; RE/BT Intro.; TT 54, 58)

3. Philosophy and the Meaning of Human Existence

There is no religion apart from man. It is man who believes and responds in faith. It is man who sins. It is man who is saved. To understand religion, then, one must understand man and his world. Philosophy is a science which asks fundamental questions about human existence. Sound theology requires a solid philosophical foundation. The philosopher asks: "What is man?" and the theologian adds: ". . . that You should be mindful of him; or the son of man, that You should care for him?"

Man does not exist apart from the world. Human existence means being-in-the-world. But we are not in the world as separate buildings against a landscape. We are essentially related to one another and to the things in the world. As we grow in awareness of our relatedness to other human beings, we experience the tension between the individual and society. We experience the polarity between self and community.

Who is the self? Even among the ancients, wise men counseled, "Know thyself." Self-knowledge would seem to be the easiest kind of knowledge to acquire, for what is closer to me than myself? Yet, it seems that the closer we are, the harder it is to see. I can understand it when someone comes to me and says: "I really don't understand you." But how do I explain the fact that I spend a lifetime trying to understand myself, only to find there is so much yet to learn? There is much in human life that is mystery.

We have a tendency to restrict mystery to God: yet, mystery permeates our world. In a pragmatic, technical world we miss much of what is significant in human existence because this world reduces mystery to problem. We have all heard about the "problem child" or the "problem parent." We even have a "God problem." But a problem is something outside us. We can examine it like an object, apply knowledge and reason, and produce a solution. However, we do not solve the child or the parent any more than we solve God. We cannot "figure them out" like a puzzle. While there is much we can know about them, there is much we will never know. This is mystery.

Mystery comes from the Greek, MYEIN, meaning to have one's eyes closed. This meaning can help us grasp the concept of mystery. Suppose you are told to look at your eyelashes. As you squint to see them, you note that you can catch a glimpse of the lashes, but you cannot see them clearly. Yet what can be closer to our eyes than our eyelashes? They are directly in front of our eyes, yet we cannot see them clearly. So it is with mystery. Mystery is part of us and all around us. Mystery is that, in human existence and in the world, which we can understand to a certain degree yet never fully comprehend. We never have it "all figured out." St. Paul was aware of this when he said: "We see now as in a dark mirror, but then we shall see face to face."

In order to get to know ourselves, we have to face

The Meaning of Human Existence

ourselves as we really are. But even to make such a statement implies that we have some kind of a relation with ourselves. As human beings, we can step outside ourselves, in a sense, and judge our behavior. It is not unusual to hear someone say: "I could have kicked myself for doing that," "I really felt proud of myself," or "I just couldn't get myself to do it." Maybe "myself" can be understood better when we make it two words: my and self. The self is mine, and I am answerable for it. We are now at the root of human responsibility. Without it, there is no freedom, no sin, no guilt, no need for forgiveness or redemption.

Only man, among all other creatures on earth, is aware of himself in this way. If we have such a relation to ourselves, we can respond to ourselves. As we learn to listen to our innermost selves and respond more appropriately, we grow in personal response-ability. We become more authentically ourselves. Self, then, is not ready-made and full blown. Self develops as my ability to respond grows.

As strange as it may sound at first, we cannot be responsible unless we are first obedient. Unfortunately, the deeper meaning of obedience is often covered over with connotations of submission to laws outside ourselves. Obedience comes from two words meaning "to hear toward." The giant radar that scans the sky can help us to grasp this deeper concept of obedience. The huge ear turns to catch all the invisible waves that ceaselessly move in its direction. The obedient person is the one who is constantly alert to the promptings of the Spirit. He knows how to listen. He is attuned to mystery.

This modern, philosophical interpretation of obedience and response-ability sheds some light on the

Gospel. Let us examine one brief scriptural passage to find out how its meaning for us can be enhanced. All of us have heard at one time or another that Jesus was "obedient unto death." This is brought out especially in the readings during Lent. Many of us, in the past, were given the impression that the Father somehow "willed" the crucifixion. We got the idea that this was the "payment" that God demanded for the sins of man. Since Jesus was obeying the "will of the Father," God somehow wanted him to die.

Now let us take another look at the obedience of Jesus. If Jesus was a human being, it would seem that the Father willed for Jesus what he wills for all other human beings, namely, that Jesus be his authentic self. He willed that Jesus stand by his values and not dilute his message. He willed that Jesus not merely pretend to be "one of the crowd." It was the will of the Father that Jesus discover the true meaning of his life and respond faithfully. The fact that threatened, insecure men put him to death was a consequence of Jesus' commitment and response-ability. His death was not the will of a God who could desire and plan for the execution of his only Son. Sound philosophical understanding can help us to see the Father as a truly loving God.

In the language of contemporary philosophy, we might say that Jesus responded to the "call of Being." In traditional terms, he was true to his "vocation" or calling in life. But a vocation is not a static state-of-life. The state-of-life is the particularized response to that call. One remains true to his vocation only as long as he continues to respond to the call of Being. As long as he knows what he stands for, as long as his value-system forms the nucleus of his activities, he is responsive to the Spirit. When he loses the vision that gives meaning

The Meaning of Human Existence

to his existence, he is unfaithful to his vocation regardless of his state-of-life.

Authenticity, we have seen, is bound up with one's values. But values are not something we acquire once and for all in completed form. As we become more and more aware of interrelationships among beings and events, our values undergo a transformation. When we enrich the meaning of our lives, our values take on an increasingly symbolic character. The deeper our values, the more satisfaction we derive from holding them. The more mature our outlook and value-system, the less we insist on having them literally satisfied.

Perhaps one example can serve as an illustration. Since Vatican Council II, Catholics have become increasingly aware of the need for "community." A Catholic who grasps the idea of community at a very deep level recognizes it as an ideal toward which we are constantly striving. He continues to hope for it, pray for it, and work for it. Holding it as a value affords security enough to persist in his efforts even when he does not find community. On the other hand, the Catholic who has not assimilated the ramifications of community is easily discouraged when he does not experience community in his parish or group. His frustration may even lead him to blame others for its absence.

The man who is not free cannot form community because he is not his own self. The group makes his decisions for him. "They" direct his life. "Everybody does it" is the standard he follows. Neither the conformist nor the rebel is free. Both are motivated by laws outside themselves. Neither the conformist nor the rebel is sure of what he stands for because he has not developed a strong personal set of values. The conformist goes along with the crowd without a question; the rebel, on the other hand, questions everything. Both miss the relatedness that belongs to community which is manifested in genuine concern for each other's welfare. This concern goes far beyond prescription or rule.

The free man is aware of whose values he is following. Developing a value system and being aware of it are characteristics of personal freedom. Whether we are conscious of it or not, we live our lives according to some pattern of behavior. There is a kind of logic, rational or psychological, that a person follows even when he is unaware of it. The free man is not only aware of the logic he is following but also sees it as his response to the truth he has come to understand. The Greek philosophers called this discourse with Being LOGOS, which is sometimes translated "word." To become free is to accept the revelation of truth. To become free is to embody the LOGOS, to make it incarnate. To become Christian, then, is to allow God's word—through Christ—to enter our private world and "become flesh."

Nevertheless, our freedom is limited. Beyond the limitations of intelligence, perception, knowledge, and experience, there are forces in society that act upon us and help determine how much of our potential we shall realize. It simply is not true that we can become anything that we wish. There is, however, something that we can do. We can relate in certain ways to the forces that act upon us. We can become aware of them, give them meaning, and take a stand in favor of those we judge to be worthwhile.

Rollo May, a philosophical psychologist, describes the way freedom works in the face of deterministic forces that act upon the individual. He uses the example of a person who wants to write a sonnet. As in the creation of any work of art, the artist must know his

The Meaning of Human Existence

material and accept its limits. Writing the sonnet means working within the relatively inflexible boundaries of rhyme and scanning. It means fitting words together according to predetermined rules. But what the poet says in the sonnet is uniquely his. And so it is with all of life. We acknowledge our human limitations. We accept the fact that the rights of others will impinge upon our external freedom. But what we do with our lives is uniquely our own.

Freedom, then, is the capacity to grow in humanness. It is the development of a response-able self and the expansion of self-awareness. It is an ever-increasing capacity to deepen our relations with our fellowmen. This freedom is not bestowed on us as a gift. We are not "born free"; our freedom must be "won anew each day." This kind of growth always demands some killing of the past, some breaking with old patterns, some changing of attitudes. Christ reminded us of this when he said: "If you would save your life, you must lose it." There is no way we can open our arms to embrace a better life when we are clutching the old one. Perhaps the words of a patient undergoing psychotherapy describe it best: "The grace of God is the capacity to change."

To the extent that we succeed in becoming free as individuals, we achieve community with others. Sometimes, people interpret community as something added on to the individual. It is looked upon as a task that lies beyond the call of duty. These people feel that concern for the community is the job of those in charge. The ordinary individual has enough to do just worrying about himself and his family. Yet, without community, we cannot be fully human. The Greeks had a word for the individual who isolated himself from others for one reason or another. IDIOS, from which we get "idiot," meant "a private person." Such an individual is walled up in his own little world, a prisoner of his own making. Furthermore, modern psychologists warn us that any family or group that is turned in on itself is not healthy.

Every community has a language which reflects the culture and values of the group. Language itself presupposes that there is an "other" who can respond. It is interesting to note that people who hate each other find it almost impossible to understand one another even though they speak the same language. When there is no awareness of human relatedness, communication is difficult. To learn to live like a human being, one must be able to communicate with other human beings. The "wild boy of Aveyron," abandoned in the wilderness as a little child, never learned to speak or even to distinguish himself from the animals until he was discovered by other human beings.

Community is not abstract society; it is concrete plurality. Collectivism can "just happen," but community must be willed. To build community, members must work continuously to shape it, reform it, and enrich it through the course of a lifetime. Collectivism proclaims an illusory path to salvation. It promises a togetherness that makes few demands on the individual. It appears to offer an escape from the pain of growth. Ultimately, it leaves the individual alone and lonely.

Community offers an opportunity for real communication. It encourages individuality, not individualism. Community enables me to say who I am and what I am about. It helps me to explain myself to myself. Without the opportunity to say who I am and what I stand for, I drift into cocktail-party chatter,

The Meaning of Human Existence

blind conformity, or bitter withdrawal. My sense of reality diminishes. When I know who I am, I find it easier to listen. Listening helps me to recognize my limits and, just as truly, empowers me to transcend myself. Listening liberates me from the fetters of my own narrow experience. Through listening, I learn that my self is part of a larger whole from which it gets its meaning and to which it can contribute. Through listening and responding, I acquire an "openness" to others and to the world.

Contemporary philosophy tells us that human existence is truly human only when it is open, responsible, obedient, and free. Just as the individual needs the community in order to become human, so the community needs the individual to keep it alive. These two dimensions, individuality and community, must be constantly balanced. The individual must not be swallowed up by the group; the group cannot be ignored by the individual. This dual aspect of existence is essential to any interpretation of the sacramental life and will be considered at greater length in a later chapter.

DOCUMENTATION

The Church has always acknowledged the importance of philosophy. Philosophy has as one of its functions the task of clarifying meanings of the language we use. So the Church, through the centuries, has used the wisdom of philosophers in an effort to make more clear and understandable the message of the Gospel and the tradition of the Church. (GS 44)

Furthermore, the bishops point out that all

aspirants to the priesthood must be well versed in modern philosophy since they will be involved in the search for solutions to problems arising from human existence. Unless one understands the deeper dimensions of human realities, he can offer only superficial help. Religious educators, also, must confront the questions that emerge from living in a world with others. Before they can bring the light of the Gospel to human events, they must be aware of the true significance of those events. Religious educators can explore the religious meaning of human existence and history more effectively if they have an understanding of the philosophical issues. They can bring a Christian meaning to existence only if they first comprehend some of the philosophical dimensions. (OT 15; GCD 74; GCD 21)

Among the depersonalizing effects of modern technology is the uprooting of traditions and history. Values that have been cherished for centuries are suddenly being challenged. Since many people drift on the surface of life, they fail to see the meaning these values have for their own lives. Mobility heightens the lack of anything stable to hold on to. Many are deprived of genuine friendship and love. (TT 36, 37, 39)

Religious educators must judge the success of their endeavors by the degree to which students are helped to see the dignity of human life and bring to this life the integrating vision of Christ. They must see how this vision can offer to a vacillating society the hope and stability of meaning, friendship, and genuine community. Religious educators must see to it that the students are helped in gradually acquiring a more mature sense of responsibility toward ennobling their own lives through constant effort. This can be done only through a continuing pursuit of authentic freedom. Within the

The Meaning of Human Existence

limits of morality and the general welfare, the individual must be free to search for truth, express his opinions, and give voice to his reflections. (TT 9, 10, 12; GE 1; GS 59)

Religious educators have the special task of doing their utmost to form men who are true lovers of freedom—men who come to decisions on their own judgment, wise men who govern their activities in the light of truth. Students must see that all freedoms are permeated with personal and social responsibility. The obedient, responsible man does not use freedom as a pretext for following his own whims. Finally, the human spirit must be cultivated in such a way that results there reflect a growth in its ability to wonder, to understand, and to contemplate. In other words, man must not lose his ability to philosophize. Wonder is the beginning of philosophy. (GE 7, 8; GS 59)

4. Belief and Faith

Every religion has its creeds or sets of fundamental beliefs. On Sundays, Catholics join their fellow worshipers in a "Profession of Faith." Publicly we affirm: "We believe in one God, the Father Almighty. . . ." What do we mean by "belief"? Does believing infer that we are reasonably sure or intellectually convinced? Or is belief a feeling we have that this is the right way for things to be?

Common usage can sometimes veil the significance of belief. When we say, "I believe it is going to rain," our belief is a deduction from the general observation that the sky is filled with dark clouds. "I believe she went to the store," indicates that we are not quite certain, but it seems likely that such is the case. The declaration, "I believe you are telling me the truth," implies that, although there may be room for doubt, I have at my disposal enough facts to make a reasonably accurate judgment. These statements illustrate shades of meaning which, while they are useful, can be misleading unless we see the relation between belief and the believer.

The word, believe, is derived from an old English word meaning "to hold dear," "to cherish." Belief has connotations of trust and confidence and an openness to receive a communication. In a story in the NEW YORKER some time ago one fictional character said: "I

Belief and Faith

would not have seen it with my own eyes had I not believed it in my own mind." In other words, coming to believe or coming to "see" requires a receptive attitude, a mind prepared to believe. When a welcoming disposition of mind is absent, a person can still acquire information, but it remains detached from his person. He lives as though he had not received the information.

What a person really "knows" is what he truly believes. For example, let us suppose that two individuals have equivalent amounts of information about the energy crisis. After acquiring this information, the first remains as wasteful and unconcerned as before. The second cuts down on his use of energy and gets his family to share his concern. Contemporary philosophers of education would hold that the first individual has not learned the information; he does not "know" the energy crisis. He does not cherish the information enough to let it affect his life. He is an unbeliever. Michael Polanyi, a well-known scientist, goes further. He says that personal knowledge is an act of commitment.

Notice that the route taken in arriving at faith is the same as that taken in arriving at wisdom as described in secular literature. In the chapter dealing with the nature of education, we noted the progress from information to knowledge to wisdom. In the area of religion, we do the same thing but we use different terms. We develop from information to belief to faith. Just as wisdom is knowledge in action, so faith is belief in action. Both indicate a personal commitment not unlike Socrates' commitment to truth and his willingness to die rather than betray that commitment.

What Christians believe stems from their trust and confidence in the person of Christ and all that he stands for. Because we believe in Christ, we hold his word dear. So when we say the words of the Creed and our hearts are not in it, we are professing convention, not creed. We are simply repeating information we have acquired. What we profess on Sundays must somehow affect our lives during the rest of the week. It must manifest itself in a lived faith.

Here is a simple test to determine the range and level of our belief. Think of the elements in the Apostles' Creed and ask: "Would I miss any one of these if it were removed from the Church's Creed?" When we cherish something, we hate to part company with it. If we, as teachers, find ourselves removing any of these fundamentals, it may be a sign we have not grasped its relationship to the other articles of faith. Or it might simply mean that we do not really understand the doctrine. In either case, we have a starting point for self-education. It is impossible to give the students a sense of the whole if we ourselves don't know how the parts fit together.

A class of adolescents might produce a variegated picture of belief if requested to complete the following mini-survey—individually or in groups.

Which of the following religious beliefs must be retained and which may be eliminated if a person who calls himself a Catholic Christian wishes to remain one? "Retain" is to be interpreted as essential to Catholic dogma. "Eliminate" is to be interpreted as non-essential, regardless of how valuable or meaningful it might be.

Belief and Faith

	Retain	Eliminate
1. The Holy Trinity	____	____
Reasons:_____		
2. Jesus as both God and man	____	____
Reasons:_____		
3. Mary, as Virgin Mother of God	____	____
Reasons:_____		
4. The resurrection and ascension of Jesus	____	____
Reasons:_____		
5. Christ's second coming as judge	____	____
Reasons:_____		
6. Presence of the Holy Spirit in the world today	____	____
Reasons:_____		
7. A church to continue Christ's work	____	____
Reasons:_____		
8. The forgiveness of sins	____	____
Reasons:_____		
9. The communion of saints	____	____
Reasons:_____		

10. The resurrection of the
    body and life after death _____   _____
    Reasons:_____

    These phrases are open and ambiguous so that the students can interpret them in their own ways. How they choose to interpret the phrases can give the teacher some indication of the climate and depth of belief. What they decide to retain or eliminate along with the reasons for their choices may uncover some gross misunderstanding of Catholic dogma. The purpose of this activity is not to rate the students' level of catholicity but to locate the deficiencies in their understanding of doctrine. Sometimes students, like teachers, can be motivated to learn when they have been confronted with their own ignorance. They frequently feel that they are well informed in matters Catholic because they are familiar with the terminology, upon which they have seldom reflected at any great length or depth.

    Genuine belief leads to its personal expression in faith. Faith is like marriage. It has connotations of loyalty and fidelity. It is a union of two persons who say: "I am with you; I am for you. I'll stay by you in good times and bad, in sickness and in health. I'll never abandon you." It means taking my partner into consideration in all the important decisions of my life. Marriage demands faith-fullness, a deep personal loyalty to the one I love.

    Marriage leaves no room for cheating on the side, for running after other lovers. Both St. Paul and the Old Testament prophets used marriage symbolism to describe the deep bond that unites God with his people. In faith, Israel and the Church are identified as "bride." Marriage is a lived experience. Merely saying

Belief and Faith 49

"I do" at one point in time will not keep two persons faithful for the rest of their lives. Marriage is a freely chosen project that must be renewed daily if it is to blossom, develop, and perdure.

So it is with faith. The faithful one refuses to be seduced by superficial attractions that promise easy success and instant happiness apart from Christ. The baptismal vow alone is no guarantee of growth in faith. The baptized must work at it, pray for it, and daily renew it. The believer has the duty to clarify and work out the content of faith as well as he can. In this, he is not alone.

Faith is no more a private affair than marriage is. Both need the support of the community to realize their full potential. Just as the individual needs the community to grow in humanness, so also the believer needs the community of believers to grow in faith. The believer's very experience of faith comes from participation in a faith-community. The faith-community promotes a sense of Christian identity, a new understanding of reality, and a genuine feeling of fellowship.

Like the individual, the community must try to clarify the content of faith. As believers, we must try to express, interpret, and grasp more adequately our Christian heritage and place it in the context of our present-day world. That is what "development of dogma" is all about. We do not discover new beliefs to add to our list. We grow in the understanding of those we hold dear. We grow in our commitment to the world and reality of the Christian tradition.

How, then, can we teach faith? We can't! If faith is a commitment to a person as in marriage, we can no more teach faith than we can teach marriage. We can only teach about marriage and about faith. Marriage and faith are lived experiences. We can learn much about the meaning of genuine Christian marriage from the witness of a loving, Christian couple. We can observe how their love of Christ and their love and respect for each other influence their relationships with other people. The witness of a mature Christian couple can help convince us that such an ideal relationship is realizable.

So it is with faith. We can tell people about faith. We can share with them the reasons why we believe. But faith is a lived response to the invitation of Christ who calls us to share in his way of life. Believing his Word means living his life. If faith makes a difference in a person's life, we can learn about faith through our contacts with mature Christians. Christians whose deep faith permeates all their interpersonal relationships can teach us most about what it means to be faithful. Attuned to the Spirit, the Christian immerses himself ever more deeply into the mystery of life with God. That is why the Church teaches that faith is the beginning in us of that eternal life in which the mysteries of God will eventually be unveiled.

If this is so, faith leaves no room for doubt. Doubt belongs on the information level. Once it is transformed into belief, it is no longer doubt. What we may have doubts about are the data that we cannot fit into our framework of belief. Modern psychological research in "cognitive dissonance" supplies evidence that a person will reject true information that goes against the grain of what he has come to believe. He can arrive at a new level of belief only after he has restructured his conceptual framework.

When we confuse the level of information with that of faith, we can make very serious errors of judgment.

Belief and Faith

Let us take a simple example from the life of a devoted married couple. The husband had noticed that, for a prolonged period of time, his wife had not been responding warmly to his expressions of love. He did not doubt her fidelity, but he did realize that something was wrong. When they finally "had it out," the husband learned that his failure to assume more responsibility for the discipline of the children irked his wife. He, of course, felt she had been doing a good job by herself. For either of these partners in marriage to have accused the other of a lack of commitment or loyalty would have been ridiculous.

Yet, we can very easily be misled into this kind of judgment in the religious domain. Let us suppose that a Catholic begins to question some interpretation of Catholic dogma. It may happen that exposure to new dimensions of truth leads him to re-examine the language of the official Church pronouncements. In his search for a deeper understanding, he may be led to raise certain issues that he feels need more clarification. He may wish to place the issues within a broader context so they are more consistent with findings in other fields. It is precisely his deep commitment to Christ and his Church that leads him to entertain doubts about certain information.

What can happen when he asks us, his fellow-believers, to help him fit his new insights into the present conceptual structures? We can ignore him. We can categorize him as a troublemaker. We can accuse him of a lack of commitment by implying that his doubts are indications of his failure to remain loyal to the Church or to Christ. To take any one of these approaches is to inhibit our own growth in faith. Jesus was very harsh on the pharisees whose "traditions" became obstacles that prevented others from acting upon God's Word.

Since a questioner cannot transform information into belief until it "makes sense" to him, we must learn to respond to the real issues. Community is enhanced when, together, we examine the issues in an effort to find what they can contribute to the development of faith. "Wherever two or three are gathered in my name, there I am in the midst of them."

Jesus prayed that we might be "one in faith"; but he did not identify it with unity of information. Had he done so, we would not be able to say that any one parish had unity in faith, much less the entire Catholic Church. Even a superficial survey would reveal differences in beliefs among persons who consider themselves dedicated Catholics. Such a condition makes development of dogma possible. Believers who have arrived at a deeper level of understanding must share their insights with those whose knowledge is not very profound. The homily during the Mass is one way that priests try to lead the parishioners to a heightened awareness of those beliefs that the Church professes.

Growth in faith is analogous to psychological development. It can be experienced on various levels; it passes through various stages. Now let us attempt an interpretation of faith on each of the three levels of meaning described in Chapter 2.

1. Sensual level: Faith is a "feeling" I have when I do something that makes me seem close to God. It is a warm feeling of security and trust.

2. Objective level: Faith is believing in "truths." The more truths I accept, the deeper my faith. Faith is

also measured by the number of commandments that I obey. G.K. Chesterton perceptively described this type of attitude toward faith. He envisions a person on this level saying something like the following about the persons of the Trinity:

"I do wish there were
four of them
So I could adore
more of them."

3. Spiritual level: Faith is a deep, personal relationship with Christ whom I accept as brother and Lord. His vision and message give meaning to my life and all of human existence. His own example gives direction to the manner in which I relate to others.

What does this mean for those engaged in religious education? First, religion teachers must interpret the message and Person of Christ in different ways to students at varying stages of cognitive and moral development. The child who experiences faith on a sensual level needs the security of being "close to Jesus" just as he needs the security of knowing that his parents love him. Strengthening trust is an appropriate task for the religion teacher working with children on this level. These children need the assurance that as long as "God is in his heaven," all will be well in their little world.

The child on the objective level is fascinated with objects, rules, and standards. Sometimes, religion teachers mistakenly suppose that students at this stage are ready for a more personal relationship with Christ. When teachers assume this position, students lose interest, not because the content is not significant, but because it is too deep for them. It is beyond the range of their present life experience. They are not ready to be guided in their conduct by their own interiorized set of values because they have not yet developed a personal value system. They are still very much guided by external rules. For example, the child's participation in the weekly liturgy probably does not stem from his personal attachment to Christ or his understanding of the Mass. In all likelihood, he goes to church because his parents tell him he must. From the attitudes and actions of adults who appreciate the liturgy, the child can learn the "fact" that the Mass is a significant activity for Catholics. He can come to understand that the words, gestures, and "objects" used during the liturgy have a profound meaning for Catholics. Hopefully, he will be stimulated to learn more about liturgy as he matures.

Once the student has developed the capacity to relate to others on a personal level, he can begin to interpret his faith on a deeper level of meaning. Nevertheless, faith as personal commitment and marriage as a symbol of the relationship between Christ and the Church will be understood only gradually. The concept must be reinforced and developed with some consistency by all the teachers involved in the religious education of students who have arrived at the personal stage of moral development. At this level, students should be challenged by the Person of Christ and confronted with his Word so that they can be helped to make a personal decision about faith.

Often, students fail to distinguish between faith and "goodness." To be a Christian is to be a "good person." A good person is one who performs observable good deeds. Their judgments indicate that they are

Belief and Faith

interpreting meaning on an objective level. For these students, what a person believes is irrelevant as far as his behavior is concerned. Even when they can understand that one can be a "good person" without being a Christian, they want to extend the name Christian, or even Catholic, to individuals who stand apart from the Christian community of believers. Confidence in their own position is somewhat shaken when it is suggested that they not call themselves Christians just because their conduct is not morally reprehensible. Their ensuing defensiveness leads them, normally, to question the meaning of "Christian." The unrest effected by this confrontation is generally great enough to make this a "teachable moment." This means that there has developed a readiness to review what being a Christian means, which is fundamental to living as a Christian.

Faith, as a free, personal response to Christ, is the mark of a mature Christian. Religious education is one way the Church endorses as a means of leading a person, gradually, to such a free decision. The believer is helped in his efforts to interpret Christ's message and apply it in his own life. As he grows in understanding and love, he begins to cherish all that God has revealed through Christ, his Son.

DOCUMENTATION

The purpose of all religious education is to enable the learner to develop a more mature, active, living faith. Just as we need the help of mature persons in our growth toward maturity, so also do we need the support of individuals who exhibit mature faith if our faith is to grow. Therefore, the faith, prayer, and example of teachers are important factors in religious education. (CD 14)

In this document, a distinction is made between two dimensions of "active faith" which is actually the same distinction as was made in the preceding pages between belief and faith. The first dimension has to do with the intellectual acceptance of the message of Christ which gives us a new vision of the world, ourselves, and God. The second aspect of faith is that of giving witness in word and deed. (TT 19)

Since it is the task of religious education to give "clarity and vigor" to faith, it would be a serious mistake for a teacher to identify essential faith with mere externals. This would, in effect, retard the growth of faith by fixating it at the objective level. It is not uncommon for individuals to say they reject Church dogma or tradition when they are actually rejecting only the familiar external which is unsatisfying to them. Religious education must help the student discern the difference. (TT 40, 87)

As we grow in our understanding of the realities and words we have inherited from the living Christian community, that tradition assumes an added significance. Communities of believers who are actively engaged in the analysis of their professed beliefs and their practice of faith, are an encouraging sign of the continuing vitality of the Church. A defensive posture that allows no questions or fears that reality will destroy faith is a sign of insecure faith or uninformed belief. (DV 8; TT 71)

Religious educators need to emphasize the relationship between faith and reason. Faith is not irrational or unreasonable. Rather, faith builds upon reason

Belief and Faith   57

as grace builds on nature. Faith takes reason beyond itself. So when we say that faith is not rational, we do not mean that it is less than reason. We do not mean that it is merely reason. Faith includes reason along with an openness to the Spirit. The obedience of faith that must characterize our relationship with God involves the whole person: reason, will, emotions. This interpretation led the bishops in council to declare that a person cannot have a mature Christian faith unless he is trained to see difficulties and master them. The believer must use his power of reason in applying his knowledge and faith in the service of justice and love. (TT 70; DV 114; GS 21)

We can be committed only to those realities we consider valuable, but transmission of values is a difficult task. In order to enable the students to develop a sound value system, religious educators must make efforts to present the Christian message with theological clarity. Teachers cannot limit themselves to providing different kinds of "religious experiences." Those engaged in religious education must aim at the ever-deepening knowledge and appreciation of our Christian heritage. (TT 52, 53; GCD 23, 24)

To teach as Jesus and the apostles did is to teach by example as well as word. Jesus never rules by force. The freedom of the student must be respected. He may be bound in conscience, but he stands under no compulsion. Faith is essentially a free response. Furthermore, an individual passes through various stages as he grows to maturity. (DH 10, 11; GCD 30)

While explication of belief must begin with simple presentations, these must be developed and applied in a manner consistent with the student's psychological and social development. (GCD 36, 38)

PART TWO

MESSAGE

To say that Christians have a message is to infer that we have something to communicate to others. Communication is not speaking or writing. It is not "show and tell." Communication is a two-way process. It includes a sender and a receiver. It always accomplishes something. It brings about a change in a person's attitude, knowledge, or behavior. A speaker does not communicate unless someone listens. When the other listens but cannot hear, looks but cannot see, there is no communication. Without someone to respond, the message withers away. "The Word falls on rocky ground."

5. Revelation and Truth

If being a person involves relatedness to others, why don't we have the same kinds of relationships with everyone? People move in and out of our lives, yet we are intimately acquainted with relatively few. Even the persons we know very well we do not always understand. How can we know and not know a person at the same time?

First, we don't come to know a person the way we arrive at knowledge of some object. We can examine an object or even take it apart to find out what "makes it tick." But a person is always more than the sum of his parts. We can make some deductions about him from observing his behavior, but a person is always more than his activity. There is a privacy about a person that not even the most empathetic friend can fathom. Unless the person reveals to us something of his inner world, we cannot get to know him as person.

So it is with divine revelation. For Christians, God is personal Being. If God is personal, he must be related to others. We can learn something about him by observing his works in nature, but unless he tells us something about himself, we cannot know him personally.

Sometimes, we hear people say that God does not "have to" reveal himself if he does not choose to do so. However, this is a gross misunderstanding of a God whose essence is love. It brings God down to the level of humans who, out of fear, insecurity, or lack of trust, fail to reveal who they really are. But "perfect love casts out fear." Only in love is a person free to reveal himself.

Even in love, however, one does not reveal everything about himself all at once. Revelation occurs gradually. Furthermore, no person can be comprehended in a single encounter. In revelation, the revealer does not merely make statements about himself; he discloses himself as he experiences himself. Only through such a revelation can a person truly BE for another.

Often we associate revelation with the spoken or written message. But revelation is not primarily a word, even though words are needed in interpreting the meaning of a revelation. If we look at the Scriptures, we see that Divine Revelation is first a deed or an event in which God discloses himself in some way. Through the inspired Word, the witnesses of these events interpret their meaning for believers.

If God reveals anything, he must reveal something about himself. Even when the revelation merely points out a relationship between God and man, it is a message from and about God. If, on the other hand, that which is gained from an experience is the knowledge, however wonderful, of how to live an authentic life without any reference to God, no revelation has been received. In revelation, God must somehow communicate his own reality. He must truly BE for the other.

Revelation also tells man about himself. In revelation, man understands himself in and through God. Therefore, to grasp one's relation to God requires that God himself be revealed in some way. This is so because one does not see his relation to God unless he

Revelation and Truth   63

sees it in God. This will be made clearer in the following section on truth which tries to show that we can discover truth only when we are already walking in the light of truth. This interpretation is similar to the theological assertion that man cannot respond to God's grace unless God first gives him the grace to respond. There can be no revelation to one who does not have the receptive attitude of faith. In wonder, the faith-filled one allows the infinite Spirit to permeate his entire awareness. "Let it be done to me according to your Word."

Since revelation and truth cannot be separated, we need to examine their meanings more closely. In the chapter on human existence, we considered how, as limited human beings, we walk in truth and untruth at the same time. Here, untruth does not refer to falsehood. Rather, it signifies deficient truth. It means that we do not know the total truth; we do not see all the possible dimensions of truth at any point in time.

Perhaps, we can get a clearer notion of truth in the image of an eclipse of the sun. When the moon is directly in front of the sun, the light from the sun is diminished. We know the sun is there, but when we look we see only the fringes, not its real center. As the moon moves across the sky, more and more of the sun is gradually revealed until the sun reaches its full brightness. But even then we do not grasp the whole sun. Much of its brightness escapes us. Its warmth is spread throughout parts of the universe that lie beyond the scope of our vision.

Revelation is like the moon's movement away from eclipse position. It is a process of unveiling, unconcealing. What it uncovers is the sun of Truth which turns darkness into light. Revelation lets the light of truth shine on all of human existence, enabling us to see its deeper meaning and bestowing on it a richer quality. "God is light and there is no darkness in him." This should help us to understand in a new way what is meant by the claim that Christ is "the way, the truth, and the life." His light shines on in the darkness, a light for the life of man.

There is never a moment when everyone in the world views the sun from the same angle or experiences its light in the same way. There can never come a time when any person, group, or nation can hoard the sunlight for itself. Sunlight is not a thing we can possess. So it is with truth. That is why we must be cautious when we say that the Catholic Church is the "one true church." There certainly is nothing wrong with the phrase as it stands. However, if we interpret this to mean that Catholics possess some "thing" called truth and that, since Catholics have "it," no other religions can possess it, then we have distorted reality.

Scripture and Revelation

The Church has always made a distinction between the limitations of biblical writers, for example, and the truth they were attempting to convey. These writers were men of their times. They interpreted events in terms of their own limited cultural and spiritual experiences. Cultural anthropologists remind us that every culture selects customs or builds traditions according to a set of deep-lying assumptions about the nature of the external world and the nature of man himself. Therefore, no society experiences all that it is possible for human beings to experience. Each culture views truth from a limited human perspective.

Revelation and Truth 65

The process by which the works of Scripture were developed and given their present form is similar to the way events are interpreted in our own day. For example, we are presently experiencing an energy crisis. When those closest to the situation first recognized it as such, they communicated the message to others. We, in turn, heard it on the radio and television; we read about it in newspapers and magazines. But how it will affect our style of life is not so obvious. Only at some future date will some interested parties be able to fit the pieces together and interpret its meaning in terms of human life. Only at some future date can we assess its significance in redirecting the course of human affairs.

If we recall that SS. Peter and Paul were no longer alive when the Gospel was put into the written form with which we are familiar, it might help us to gain a proper perspective. The spoken words and deeds of Jesus came first. The apostles, after the resurrection, proclaimed the Good News of Christ. Eyewitnesses recollected Jesus' words, life, and deeds. They developed an oral tradition. Even Paul, when he established churches in various parts of the then-known world, had no written documents to leave with his converts. Since he could not remain with all these Christian communities at the same time, he began to write letters to them. Some of his letters are among the earliest of the New Testament writings.

Students should not be given the impression that the evangelists walked around with a scroll of papyrus tucked under one arm just waiting to jot down some sacred words or produce an account of some memorable event. When this idea is conveyed, the words of Jesus can become a source of agitation, especially to adolescents. They can experience as contradiction statements like: "I am the light of the world" coupled with: "Learn of me for I am meek and humble of heart." A Jesus who appears boastful and proud can disturb them deeply. Reminding them that Jesus is also Son of God is not very helpful because it does not get to the root of their problem. An understanding of how the Gospels were produced can be more rewarding than an exhortation to have faith.

We have no way of checking the exactness of the details or the sayings recorded in the Gospels. What we do know with certainty is that all those things that were recorded assumed their final form within a community of believers, the Church. Everything said about Jesus was colored by the early Church's faith in Christ as Messiah and Lord. It is important that students see the relation between Church and Gospel. They frequently claim they can be "Christian" without a church. Often, they do not realize that they would not have a Gospel had it not been produced within the Church. Were there no Church, it is hardly likely that many of them would have heard of Jesus. If Christ lives today, it is because the Body of Christ is the same "yesterday, today, and forever."

The Church as Revelation

From the very beginning of the Church, the teachings handed down by the apostles were developed in the community as believers achieved new levels of understanding and experienced new dimensions of faith. Through all the changes in its outer forms, the essence of that teaching has remained unchanged. We believe this because Jesus promised that his Spirit would re-

Revelation and Truth

main with us and bring to our minds all that Jesus taught us. We shall not, as community, be led astray. The word used to describe this effect of the Spirit in the Church is infallibility.

Because this work is so misunderstood, Catholics often make unwarranted claims under its aegis. To think of it only in terms of papal pronouncements is inadequate and misleading. One gets the impression that the Roman pontiff can be pope apart from the rest of the believing community. Outside that community, his word would be as effective as that of a king without a kingdom. Infallibility does not mean that the pope has some kind of supernatural powers of discernment that are not available to the rest of mankind. It does not mean that what a pope says is always the most comprehensive, the most clear presentation of truth that we can ever discover. The office of pope is no guarantee that the incumbent has broken through the limitations of his own cultural tradition or spiritual experience.

This is not to deny that the pope has very special authority and power in the Church community. It does deny that his chief role is to think up new rules for Catholics to obey. His function is much more important than rule-making. The pope, as "one who serves," has the indispensable task of preserving the Church in a unity of faith. Unity of faith is not the same as conformity in speech. It is never found without the vision which constitutes its hope and the service which marks its love. The Church, it is said, is like a bridge leading from the present, unfulfilled state of God's Kingdom to that future condition when God will become "all in all." Seen in this light, the very title of the pope assumes a deeper significance. The Roman pontiff is always a "bridge builder."

Like all Christians, the pope must be obedient; he must "listen toward" the Spirit (see chapter 3). He, along with bishops and the rest of us believers, must be open to all aspects of truth which can lead to a more profound understanding of our Christian heritage. For infallibility extends to the bishops in council and to the People of God acting in unison. It is not the duty of the pope alone to watch over the content of that heritage. Truth is a communal discovery, and without dialogue the written word can separate rather than unite men. Listening to each other, we learn who we are. In dialogue, our corporate identity is strengthened.

The late Cardinal Bea expressed the view that infallibility is a marvelous instrument for preventing the Catholic Church from becoming a national church. If bishops and other mature believers were to abdicate their responsibility with respect to the content of revelation, decisions that affect us all might very well be made within the cultural framework of a particular nation. The Church has had to pay a high price for having failed to make a distinction between the content of revelation and its expression within a particular society or culture. Peoples in various nations rejected the "Good News" when it was presented as a package wrapped in European customs. The gift of infallibility carries with it Christ's promise that we, as a believing community, will not ultimately confuse the medium with the message.

Even from a merely human point of view, infallibility of the community as a whole makes sense. Remember, infallibility is a negative term. It assures us that, as a community of believers honestly searching for the truth, we shall not be led astray in matters of faith and morals. Modern research in group problem-solving

Revelation and Truth

reveals that groups generally produce solutions that are qualitatively superior to individual solutions. Diversified groups seem to have a built-in correction mechanism for detecting error. Since, in a group, more dimensions of a problem are brought to light, the group can suggest better alternatives. Furthermore, groups can foresee more of the consequences that a particular decision might have. So, when dedicated Christians genuinely desiring to know the truth join forces in reinterpreting the message of faith, they can have confidence that any errors that might lead them away from the original message of Jesus will be detected by the Church.

Faith and Miracles

To detect God's presence in events demands the openness of faith. Human reason is never a threat to faith because our faith is not unreasonable. To see the Spirit working in the Church requires no directly observable miracles. To be able to say that the pope had a "direct line" of communication with God would be comforting, but not necessary. Yet sometimes people feel that they would have a deeper faith if they could experience some type of miracle like that which would solidify their faith. Before we can evaluate such a position, we must examine closely the meaning of miracle. We do know that there were times when Christ chose to reveal something about himself or his Father through miracles. Yet, he had words of scorn for the sign-seekers, the miracle-hunters.

The Gospels show clearly that Jesus condemned as an "evil and unfaithful generation" those people who were always looking for displays of divine power. For those calculating people, God had to show himself in some extraordinary way. He had to prove himself in happenings that would satisfy the physical senses. The miracle-hunters demanded that God lay aside the ordinary laws of nature in order to convince them of his power. To them, the significant aspect of a miracle lay not in the action of God but in the sensible phenomena, the big show, the magic.

How, then, are we to interpret Jesus' miracles? The word miracle comes from the Latin MIRARI, which means "to wonder at." So even in a non-religious sense, a miracle is defined as an event that causes astonishment or surprise. It is a happening that inspires "wonder." The real difference between the believer and the unbeliever becomes evident in the way each interprets the event. Let us take an example from the Gospels. For the apostles and disciples, an empty tomb meant that Jesus had truly risen from the dead; for those who had never accepted Jesus, it meant that Christ's body had been stolen.

We should not think that the followers of Jesus saw and heard things that could not be witnessed by the enemies of Jesus. Those who hated Jesus saw the same public deeds and observed the same events that the disciples witnessed. Unbelief prevented many people from seeing the divine reality that brought about these events. Lack of faith prevented them from getting the message revealed through such activity. So witnessing a miracle is no guarantee of a stronger faith.

For believers, God is already present in events that occur in the world. For them, the miracle is one of those events that stands out from the others in a distinctive and significant way. God acts in the event in a

Revelation and Truth

special way. God is the one who brings it about and intends to achieve some special end through it. The miracle is one way in which God's presence and activity can be made known. But it is not a "proof" that will satisfy the sign-seeker. While there are factors that cannot be accounted for on the natural level, the elements in a miracle are not composed of magic.

For believers, the essence of the miracle is to be found in God's presence and the way he reveals himself in the event. For the "evil and unfaithful generation," the miraculous element is the spectacular, publicly observable happening. For the believer, the most important dimension of a miracle, God's presence, is not publicly demonstrable. It does not demand exceptional breaks in the laws of nature. When Christians focus on the external phenomena of miracles instead of God's presence, they can unwittingly foster negative attitudes toward faith. Rejection of miracles as superstitious and outmoded may very well be a reaction against an inadequate interpretation of miracle.

Young children cannot grasp the concept of revelation or miracle. If miracles are stressed at this stage, children may pick up notions of magic. Jesus may come to be seen as a "superstar" who went about accomplishing amazing feats for no particularly profound reasons. Children at this level can, however, learn that nature reveals something about God and his care for us. Children have the capacity to understand some of the basic content of revelation, e.g., that God became man and lived among us teaching us how to be good.

Children who interpret events on an objective level cannot grasp the broader concept of truth. They can learn only true statements; they know only "facts." Miracles are obvious "proofs" that Jesus is God. Only when students can interpret events on a spiritual plane can they grasp the concept of personal revelation. They can understand that nothing is revealed unless the recipient welcomes revelation.

In summary, persons who love are moved to reveal themselves to the ones they love. The God whom Christians acknowledge is both loving and personal. He reaches out through people, events, and deeds to show us who he is. To the community of believers who accept the revelation of God which comes through Christ is given the Spirit of God to direct its efforts and protect it from slipping into the darkness of error.

DOCUMENTATION

In the course of human history, God made himself known through personal communication. Through certain events and people, God gradually unfolded his design for the fulfillment of human existence. He revealed himself as one who invites us into community with him. He calls us to an intimate, personal relationship with him. (TT 16; GCD 10; DV 2)

God did not reveal everything about himself all at once. Patiently, God prepared the people, Israel, for the complete message which found its full human expression in Jesus Christ. Since the events and deeds through which God made himself known were open to all kinds of interpretations, God always made use of human words to reveal the significance of an event. Word and deed belong together. (TT 47; GCD 11, 37; RE/BT 1)

The early Christian community preserved in writing the deeds and words of Jesus. The message of the

Revelation and Truth

Old Testament finds its fulfillment in the New. All parts of the message are interrelated, and it is important to recognize the harmony of content. The Church is called to proclaim fully this message of Christ and to preserve it intact. The Church is not above the Word it serves and must take care to interpret this Word authentically. (TT 16, 17; GCD 38, 39; DV 8)

Through the centuries, the Church moves forward constantly toward the fullness of divine truth, striving to realize the Word of God more completely. In order to accomplish this, the bishops and all the faithful must cherish and profess the heritage of faith in community. Through common effort, they must adapt it to new problems and try to arrive at a new understanding of the content of revelation. (DV 10)

Such understanding is developed through prayer, reflection on Sacred Scripture, and practice of our faith. Understanding is furthered when we examine the genuine human moral values in society and place them within the Christian context. Dialogue with the official teachers of the Church community is essential to growth in faith. (GCD 45)

We must seek to interpret human life in our age and the signs of the times in the light of the revelation we have received. We must make the content of the message intelligible to men of all times. Jesus spoke in the idiom of his day. So the Church, too, must use the methods and language of our own day to proclaim the message. (DV 4; GCD 37; TT 18)

We cannot merely repeat ancient doctrine because the words have undergone a change in meaning. Within the fundamental unity of faith, there is room for a plurality of cultural differences, forms of expression, and theological views. (GCD 13)

Allowing for differences in expression, we still hold that, in the last analysis, all attempts at reformulating the message come within the jurisdiction of the teaching authority of the Church. The pope, as universal guardian and teacher, has the supreme task of confirming his brothers in faith. A footnote to the CONSTITUTION OF THE CHURCH, explains that the case of a pope defining something apart from his fellow bishops is "a purely imaginary one." The pope can truly BE pope only within a believing community. (LG 25)

6. Trinity and Creation

The Christian religion is distinguished by its worship of a triune God. This doctrine is at the root of all other dogmas and holds them in unity. Yet, the concept of Trinity appears irrelevant to many Christians. The trinitarian formula does not help them to understand God better nor does it seem to shed light on human existence. The term does not have the warm emotional connotations of words like Father, Jesus, Savior. Trinity conjures up impersonal images of isosceles triangles and three-leaf clovers. Believers accept the "fact" of three Persons in God, but it very often leaves them unmoved.

Yet God never reveals anything simply to supply us with information. Revelation is never irrelevant; our interpretations of it might be. In the past, remnants of philosophical arguments found their way into Catholic catechisms. Children were burdened with unassimilated information about three Divine Persons in one divine nature. Such descriptions of God were too far removed from the life and experience of the students to be meaningful. The mental gymnastics involved in trying to force three "persons" into one skin could produce only a caricature of God. This intellectual activity proved to be unrewarding and unenlightening.

However puzzling the language chosen by the original Christian community, it was meant to be an interpretation, a clarification. The early Christian community believed that God who created the heavens and the earth had lived among them in a particular man and was still with them guiding them as a community. The only concept that could explain such an experience was that of a triune God. This is the way they expressed in human language their understanding of the very mystery of God as he is in himself.

No matter how complex the concepts we develop to describe God's nature, we know that, in the last analysis, God is always "more" than our descriptions of him. Nevertheless, we can enrich our own life of faith by pondering on this fundamental mystery, the Holy Trinity. Contemporary works in ontology provide some valuable insights. Ontological studies deal with Being, the source of beings.

The book of Exodus in the Old Testament contains an account of Moses' encounter with Yahweh. When Moses asks about the self-identity of this God who addresses him, he receives his answer in terms of Being. God replies: "I am Who am." In other words, God is Holy Being. God causes to be whatever comes into being. God lets-be whatever comes into existence. God is not just a being among beings. He is not even a supreme being. He is Being itself.

Turning to the Gospel of John, we come across an incident in which Jesus makes a claim to divinity in terms of Being. When the Jews inquired how he could possibly have known their father Abraham, Jesus responded: ". . . before Abraham came to be, I AM." Jesus was nearly stoned to death for this statement. For to say "I AM" was to identify himself with Holy Being. He was saying that all things come into being through him. This is why in the liturgy we Christians

Trinity and Creation

proclaim that all things were made ". . . . through him, with him, and in him."

Leaving out such difficult concepts as circuminsession, spiration, and procession, we can still make use of the ideas of traditional Christian theology in trying to understand our triune God. What follows is simply a rephrasing of the traditional "explanations."

The Father might be described as primordial or ultimate Being. He has always been "Father." In other words, there was never a "time" when he lived in isolation and only at some later date generated the Son. The Father is and always has been the source of Being, the source of life and love. Human existence can find its truest and deepest meaning only when it focuses on its source in the Father. That is why Jesus was so caught up in doing the "will of the Father." That is why he looked forward to his return to the Father. Jesus knew where the well-springs of life really are, and he wanted us to know this, too.

The Son is "expressive" Being. As LOGOS or Word, he is the very expression of the Father. He is the agent of the Father in creation and re-creation. The Scriptures continually remind us that it is through God's Word that everything in creation comes to be. It is also through his Word that Being is expressed in all creatures and, in a very special way, in human beings among whom the Word "pitched his tent." If we are called as Christians to become like Christ, it means that we must allow our Father to express himself through us. Christ raised human existence to a new awareness because he let the light of Being shine through his person. Christ, in turn, challenges us to "let your light shine before men."

The Holy Spirit is unitive Being. It is through the

Spirit that the unity of Being is maintained and strengthened. It is through the Spirit that beings who have lost their way are brought back into the light of Being. The Spirit unites beings with the source of Being. That is why Christians pray: ". . . in the unity of the Holy Spirit." Even though Holy Being shows himself in all beings, we may miss it altogether. To say that a human person is "spiritual" is to say that he has the capacity for an openness to Being. He has the capacity to perceive Being in beings. In chapter two, we considered three levels of meaning. Only the person on the spiritual level can probe this deepest meaning of his own existence.

But even when we say that God is Being or God is Love, we are so conditioned by our language that we might still think of God as static, unmoving essence. We know that God gives of himself. Self-giving is always a sign of life, and life is movement. In the Old Testament, God pleads with his people to "choose life." Jesus pointed out that our God is a "God of the living." And according to St. Athanasius: "The glory of God is a man fully alive." If it pleases God that man come alive, then God himself must be utter and ultimate alive-ness. God as Being-alive expresses himself in dynamic self-communication and creativity. God must be alive in this way because he is truly Being-in-Love.

We know from our own human experience what being in love does to a person. Being in love makes a person come alive in a new way. Being in love moves the lover to give of himself, to share with the other. Being in love leads a person to give expression to his inner being. Only when we allow the other enough freedom to be genuinely present to us in this way can he truly BE for us. As Gabriel Marcel described it: "When

Trinity and Creation

the other is truly present to me, he makes me more myself than I would have been had he not revealed himself."

Being in love, then, makes two people one in such a way that each one separately is more than he was before because he now shares more being, so to speak. The life-giving element is the love itself. The new life that each one experiences does not depend on something the loved one has attained or done. We are lovable because "God first loved us." We are the human expression of Being-in-Love.

Being-in-Love describes the interrelations among the Father, Son, and Spirit. The love of the Father pours itself out in a divine activity that beautifully and perfectly expresses all that the Father is. This personal expression of the Father's love we have come to call the Son of God. Between the Son and the Father there has always been an undivided, personal unity—the Spirit of the Father and the Son. Each Person is related to the other and united to each other in love. So the Holy Trinity is the primordial community, the model and source of human community.

It is in interrelatedness through expressive love and unity that we are truly the "image and likeness of God." Older philosophies defined man as a "rational animal." Since theology builds on philosophy, theologians assigned this divine likeness to the domain of human rationality. So we grew accustomed to saying that man is like God because man has the power to reason. But infants and young children cannot reason. Many human beings never attain the full use of reason. Furthermore, in the realm of religious dogma, we are reminded that full use of reason without a disposition of faith is a dead-end street.

So there must be something more fundamental in our humanity in which the divine likeness resides. We noted in chapter three that modern philosophy defines human existence in terms of relations. We can exist as human beings only if we are consciously related to others. To BE is to be-with. Being-with is not a matter of being-alongside others, like buildings against a landscape. It is not "togetherness." Being-with is an attitude of caring which springs from the awareness that we all have the same source of Being. We all have the same loving Father.

Being-with does not mean that we should never be alone. Rather, it points out that, even in solitude, we are related to others. We need solitude in order to come to an awareness of our relatedness to others and to deepen our sense of relatedness. St. Therese of Lisieux spent her adult life in a cloister, secluded from the outside world. Yet, she was named by the Church as "Patroness of Missionaries." Why? Therese, in her solitude, never forgot her relatedness to others. She was intensely aware of being-with others in this world. And because she cared so much, she poured out her love in prayer and sacrifice for the success of those who preached the Word of God.

We are all called to be this type of saint. Jesus himself challenged us: "Be perfect as your heavenly Father is perfect." Unfortunately, we very often interpreted this to mean building up some kind of super-human structure adorned with various "virtues." When we realized the impossibility of ever arriving at such a Tower of Babel, we were counseled not to take the Word of the Gospel literally. But if we think in terms of relatedness, the Father's own self-giving can serve as our model. In this sense, then, our perfection must lie in the

Trinity and Creation 81

continuous outpouring of ourselves in creative love. It must lie in forging a bond of unity with others. Our perfection then must reside in arriving at an ever-deeper awareness of our unity in Being. Our perfection must express itself in the creation of community.

We know that faith and hope "will pass away," but our relatedness to others, our participation in the same source of Being will continue forever. This is one reason for the Christian's acceptance of the communion of saints. We know that those who have gone before us and those who will come after us are related to us in Being. We can still feel close to a friend who has died because the bond of unity is not broken. "Love," the Word of God proclaims, "is stronger than death."

To talk about saints or any other kinds of beings in the world is to talk about creation. It is no longer adequate to think of creation as an act that God performed at the beginning of time. Creation did not end "on the sixth day." Creation is an on-going activity through which things and people are newly created. Man and his world are not finished products. We are not yet all that we can be.

Since creation is a continuing process, it includes the notion of God's Providence. To speak of Divine Providence is to assert that God's constant creative and sustaining power is at work in our world. Belief in Divine Providence says that creation has a purpose; it is headed in a definite direction. St. Thomas explains it as an ordered movement into fuller and richer kinds of Being. Providence, however, is not the same as evolution, regardless of how valuable the scientific theory may be.

Belief in Divine Providence stems from human experience. Throughout salvation history, God continues to reveal himself in words and "marvelous deeds." Certain events or happenings in our lives give us a heightened sense of Being. They make us more aware of God's action in our lives. They rejuvenate us, giving us a sense of Being more fully alive. They give us hope. Hope is not mere wishful thinking. Rather, it is the confidence that is born out of the knowledge that life is, indeed, meaningful. We do not roam aimlessly through an absurd world.

Sometimes, those of us who were baptized as infants and brought up in a community of faith do not realize how painful a life is without meaning. We do not sense the genuine agony, the ANGST, of one who must search all by himself for the meaning of human existence. Perhaps the words of Dag Hammarskjold will help us appreciate the value of a meaningful existence. "What I ask for is absurd: that life shall have a meaning. What I strive for is impossible: that my life shall acquire a meaning. I dare not believe, I do not see how I shall ever be able to believe: that I am not alone." He writes later: ". . . at some moment I did answer YES to Someone . . . and from that hour I was certain that existence is meaningful and that, therefore, my life, in self-surrender, had a goal" (*Markings*, p. 205). He begins to pray to Father, Son, and Holy Spirit. And in the end, just before he died, he was able to write about his experience of a life lived on a new level of meaning (*Markings*, p. 222):

Is it a new country
Or did I live there
Before Day was?
. . . .

Trinity and Creation

The seasons have changed
And the light
And the weather
And the hour.

But it is the same land.
And I begin to know the map
And to get my bearings.

But "getting one's bearings" is a matter neither of fate nor of Calvinistic predestination. Fate says that every single happening has been determined ahead of time by God. Fate excludes free will and human responsibility. We know that God does not wish evil; therefore, it is unchristian to attribute to "God's Will" that which is really the consequence of human shortcomings. Predestination, in the narrow sense, says that God chooses some individuals and rejects others. It says that he has already marked out some for heaven and some for hell, as though he were under pressure to fill some kind of quota in both "places."

We have not advanced very far beyond this kind of thinking when we ask: "How can a good God SEND anyone to hell?" What we are implying in this question is that, in the end, God makes the decision. It implies that the individual has little or no say in the matter. Naturally, since God made us so that we might one day enjoy complete happiness with him, it is difficult to understand how he could send someone to hell. In fact, he does no such thing.

In his account of the last judgment, Jesus says to those who stood condemned: "When I was hungry . . . when I was thirsty . . . when I was naked . . . in prison . . . you did nothing to alleviate my distress. You did not care enough to reach out to help me." And the guilty condemn themselves by their own response: "When did we see you hungry or thirsty or naked or in prison?" And that is precisely the point! They never bothered to look for him; that is why they failed to recognize him in their midst. Whatever their excuses, they never looked deeply enough into other persons to see the image of the God in whom we all "live and move and have our being."

St. Thomas held that, at the moment of judgment, we are given our final choice. We are given a last chance to decide, once for all, the ultimate meaning of our lives. We can find our fulfillment in Christ or we can seek it apart from him. "He who is not with me scatters." As much as God desires our salvation, he will not force the issue. St. Augustine teaches that God, who created us without our cooperation, will not save us without our help. Even during a very trying moment, when people were walking away from Jesus, he refused to use force. He simply asked the apostles: "Will you also go away?"

The final choice looks deceptively simple. After all, how can anyone fail to choose Christ in such a situation? We have to remember that we see only what we are prepared to see. In this sense, all our life is a preparation for seeing Christ face-to-face. We have all kinds of signs along the way. We catch a glimpse of him in some event. We sense his presence in a personal relationship. And each time we acknowledge his presence, we get to know him a little better. Then, when the final choice comes at the moment of death, we choose Life because we have chosen it all along.

What if, in life, we have chosen only ourselves? What if we have refused to look beyond our own needs,

Trinity and Creation

our own satisfactions, our own convenience? If we have not recognized the Being in which our lives were immersed, we will not be prepared to see it in the end. In that final moment, it is hardly likely that we shall be able to break the habit that we developed during an entire lifetime. It seems likely that we shall choose only what we have made ourselves capable of choosing—ourselves. We shall not recognize Christ then any better than we did in our lifetime. Christ will appear as a stranger. How can we seek union with someone we do not know? How can we choose Life when our whole life was simply a matter of not dying? This is the real human tragedy: those who refuse Life in this world choose death in the next.

We can see, then, that salvation is not something that takes place only at the end of our lives. Sometimes, we hear Catholics saying that they want their sins forgiven so that they can get to heaven in the end. They seem to identify forgiveness of sin with salvation. But salvation, while it includes forgiveness, means much more. We know, for example, that Yahweh forgave his people Israel over and over again; yet, they still waited for a savior. They awaited salvation. If salvation were limited to forgiveness of sin, then Yahweh was saying something like: "I'll forgive you, but you'll have to wait around for about two thousand years for it to take effect!" Such conduct is, indeed, incomprehensible.

The New Testament does not identify forgiveness of sin with salvation either. Jesus is the savior. Jesus brings salvation; Jesus is salvation. He brings forgiveness, it is true, but he brings much more. Jesus said of John the Baptist, the greatest prophet of the Old Testament, "Even the least in the Kingdom is greater than

John." Certainly, this cannot mean that God was slower to forgive John his failings. John never lived to receive the full message of revelation. John never learned about the new way of life to which Christians are called. John never shared the marvelous vision of Christ about God's plan for human fulfillment in his Kingdom.

Let us now consider some of the dimensions of salvation. First, in all religions salvation means a freeing of man from his own estrangement. Salvation reunites man with the sacred. We use the word estrangement in talking about divorce. It conveys the notion of an interpersonal relationship that has deteriorated. Two persons who were intimately united have now become strangers to one another. Salvation, it is true, brings the stranger into harmony with himself and with others. But salvation is more.

Salvation is the positive experience of sharing in divine Being in what can only be described as a rebirth. God raises us up to a new life, a whole new way of living and experiencing the world. He enables us to view everything with the eyes of Christ. Salvation is like the experience of the prodigal son who suddenly realizes he does not have to spend the rest of his life among the swine. It is like the feeling he experienced when his father's welcome brought him to a new awareness of how deeply his father really loved him and how sorrowfully he had awaited his return. It is like the joy of the prodigal who could now say: "This is where I belong. This is what my life is all about. I don't have to wander any more pursuing a happiness that will not last. I can find this and much more in my father's house . . . 'pressed down and running over'."

Jesus hinted at this aspect of salvation when he no-

Trinity and Creation 87

ticed his followers' jubilant spirits at having been successful in casting out devils. "Don't rejoice so much," he said, "that devils are subject to you as that your names are inscribed in heaven." In other words, the joy of knowing that we are already experiencing the love of the Father, Son, and Spirit which is the source of our power over evil far surpasses any successes we may experience in our struggle against evil.

Once again, let us examine the way philosophy affects theology. We associate salvation with freedom, and this is the way it should be. But the problem develops because we look at freedom from only one perspective. We talk about freedom-FROM and we forget freedom-FOR. Our own society furnishes enough tragic examples of people with a high degree of freedom from external limitations who have not yet attained freedom-FOR. Their lives lack direction and commitment. They fail to see that we remove obstacles so that we can arrive at a specific destination. Instead, they spend their lives demanding the removal of the roadblocks without ever asking where the road leads.

Such a state of aimless wandering is analogous to the situation of a man who is released from a concentration camp only to be told that he must spend the rest of his life wandering in the wilderness. Isolated from others, a prey to wild animals, he experiences more of a threat to his existence than he did in the minimal life within the confines of the camp. No matter which course he follows, he ends up in the same place with only increased frustration. Jesus told a parable that is closely related to this. He said that an unclean spirit went out of a man. After a while the spirit returned and "found the house empty, swept, and tidied." So the spirit called together seven spirits who were more evil than himself, and they moved into the empty house of the man "and the last state of that man was worse than the first."

Modern psychology tells us that people often complain about feeling "empty." This emptiness is a total lack of relatedness to others, a feeling of not belonging. The empty person feels powerless to direct his own life or to influence the world around him. Such emptiness diminishes life and may lead to violence. Often, the empty person is the "liberated" individual who has tasted "all that life has to offer." After traveling a long way on his road of "freedom," he finds himself lonely and alone.

Christ is truly a savior because he fills our empty houses with the gracious gift of his presence and refuses to let us be victimized by the destructive forces surrounding us. His power transforms us not only in our psyche but also in our very being. He leads us out of the wilderness of aimless wandering. He points out the direction we must go to find genuine fulfillment. Christ cannot live in us without forming in us his relation to the Father. In so doing, he makes us "sons of God." That is why an ancient liturgical prayer proclaimed: "God became man so that we might become God."

On the way to becoming who we truly are, faith lights our way. In faith, we perceive the Reality behind appearances. As Jesus said to the adulterous woman: "Your faith has been your salvation." We make progress in this way of salvation by participating in all those events which unveil that Reality: revelation, sacred rites, sacraments, direct experience. Salvation is a continuing process that is experienced again and again as the Church endeavors to make present through the liturgical cycles the Salvation Event. In faith, we

Trinity and Creation 89

allow Jesus to BE for us what he truly is—SAVIOR.

A creature lives the way of salvation when he sees himself in the light of Being. For to be a creature is to acknowledge human existence as both a gift of Being and an accountability to Being. To come to terms with our creatureliness, we must acknowledge that, although we are not self-sufficient, we are empowered to attain fuller being. And for this we are answerable to God. This idea is tied in with Jesus' words: "Trade until I return." In other words, Jesus is telling us that, when we are children, we live our lives on a certain level. Our existence is not as rich as it can be. As we grow into adulthood, we are expected to enrich our own lives and the lives of those with whom we "trade." Not to be concerned with greater possibilities, with deeper values, with a richer existence, is to "bury our talents."

There is, of course, no reason to suppose that creation begins and ends with man. As man looks out into the vastness of space and possible other worlds, he wonders if there might not be creatures who surpass man in being. There is talk about the possibility of highly developed civilizations on other galaxies. It is hardly scientific to disclaim anything just because all the evidence is not in. So to limit existence to human beings and make man the measure of all things is narrow and parochial.

In our sophistication, we Christians are sometimes embarrassed at the mention of angels. Angels are so much like an artifact from another age. We don't seem to need them anymore. So we explain them away as mere figures of speech. Yet angels appear throughout both the Old and New Testaments; therefore, they cannot be dismissed lightly. This is not to say we understand them completely. But it does mean that simply talking them out of existence is not very helpful.

Whatever the meaning of angel, it is important that we not lose our sense of wonder, our openness to Being which expresses itself in countless ways that we cannot even imagine. "Eye has not seen nor ear heard." Sometimes the word angel is used in the Bible to imply an activity of some higher order of beings. At other times, the concept seems to represent God's action or self-communication. The Scriptures speak of rebellious and proud angels. What we can learn from this account is that pure spiritual being is no guarantee against sin. Spiritual pride is always destructive. On the positive side, the concept of angel stands for the unity and order of the whole of creation in the conscious and free service of Being.

Because Trinity, creation, and salvation are important, we sometimes overexpose children to them. In our genuine concern to lead children to a more mature faith, we subject them to so much terminology that, by the time they are ready to understand the concepts, they are tired of hearing it all. The concepts are no longer challenging or new. It is more reasonable, as the bishops remind us, to share with students only as much as they are prepared to understand. It is important, though, that they be helped to know that as they grow into adulthood they will gradually be introduced into the richer and deeper layers of the Christian heritage. It is not wrong to keep them yearning for that "more" which mature Christian adults manifest in their lives.

Naturally, a child on the sensual level does not perceive Father as life-giver because he does not perceive his own father as a life-giver. The child usually interprets daddy as the one who works to earn money for food and clothes. He provides for the family's physical

Trinity and Creation

comfort and security. Father might be the one who spanks him when he is bad. Children can grasp the idea that daddy does this because he loves them and because it is important to keep the family together. Children know they could never make it on their own, a notion that is essential to community.

Once he can interpret experiences on an objective level, the student can learn respect for "things"—including people. It is not possible for the pre-adolescent who is uncomfortable with his own body to relate to others in any personal or spiritual way. He relates in very concrete ways, like slugging the other guy or "accidentally" shoving the girl he likes. He measures his progress on the way to salvation by the number of "good deeds" he has done. These deeds are his contribution to the formation of community. Community is willed, and good deeds are the only way this student knows to show that he wants to belong. To try to force him to go beyond these concrete acts at this stage in personal development is a practice in futility.

The students on the third level of cognitive and moral development can grasp the spiritual dimension of religious concepts. When they are introduced to any concept, however, they must be enabled to see how the new concepts are related to what they have already learned. They may need much help in learning what these religious concepts mean in terms of their own personal fulfillment.

We have seen that the Triune God revealed through Christ is the supreme model for human community. Community, then, is not something extra that we are free to choose or reject. Community is indispensable to genuine human existence. Only in a true community is there such an atmosphere of trust and letting-be that a person feels free to reveal his inner being. When this happens, relatedness is strengthened and being is expanded. Establishing the conditions that allow a person to BE what he truly is in the light of Being is to walk in the way of salvation.

DOCUMENTATION

In the history of God's dealing with men, God reveals himself as the one true personal God. The Old Testament revelation was a preparation for the mystery of the Trinity revealed in the person, words, and works of Jesus. Jesus showed himself as the eternal and divine Son of God. He revealed more fully the Father, and he made known a third Person, the Holy Spirit, whom the Father and he sent to remain with his "little flock." (RE/BT 1)

Through the Spirit, Jesus calls all believers to such a close relationship with him that we become sons of God, also. Religious educators must create learning situations in which an ever-increasing awareness of the Triune God is fostered. Since this mystery is central to our faith, it is important that students be motivated to develop a lifelong, developing intimacy with the three Divine Persons. (RE/BT 1)

When we reflect on the mystery of creation, we must relate the creative activity of God "in the beginning" to God's continuing activity in the history of man's salvation. The world that was created out of nothing is the same world in which Christ redeems us and leads us in the way of salvation. Jesus is the greatest of created beings. As the "firstborn" of creation, he

Trinity and Creation 93

brings us new life. All things come together in unity through him. Since Christ is also the firstborn from the dead, he offers all of us the hope of eternal life. (RE/BT 5; GCD 50, 51)

In Jesus, we are related to all history and all men. Therefore, creation should not be taught in isolation from other salvation events. God is still among us and will bring his saving work to final completion when there will be a "new heaven and a new earth." Christians allow the glory of God to shine through creation when they develop their human capacities and take advantage of opportunities for personal growth. (RE/BT 5-6)

Since salvation takes place in human experience in this world, religious educators must be careful not to create too wide a gap between:

God's plan of salvation	and	human aspirations and longings
the history of salvation	and	human history
the Church	and	other human communities
God's revealing action	and	man's experience
supernatural gifts and charisms	and	human values

While the concepts in the first column are not identical with those in the second, they are inseparably linked together. (GCD 8)

Man was created "in the image and likeness of God." God did not create him as a solitary. Man in his innermost nature is a social being. He cannot live or develop his potential unless he relates to others. Christians must make an effort to learn the deepest meaning and value of creation, including human existence, and to help each other in this effort. In this way, we relate all of creation to the praise of God. (LG 12; GS 36)

Jesus taught us that the supreme meaning of human life is linked with doing the Father's will. This is brought about when, in the light of the Spirit, we continually move toward greater communion with him. Although Christ is at the center of the history of salvation, he is always there with Father and Spirit. These three give the Christian message its unique characteristics; therefore, religious educators should never neglect their close relationship. (GCD 41)

The history of salvation is identical with the history of the way and the plan by which God, as Trinity, reveals himself to man. It is the history of the way God reconciles and unites man with himself after man has turned away in sin. It is the history of the life, death, and resurrection of Christ who taught us his way of life. All three Persons of the Trinity must be acknowledged as authors of the plan of salvation. As we contemplate this truth, we can grow to cherish with filial love the Father, Son and Holy Spirit. (GCD 47)

7. Sin and Evil

Often we hear people say: "If God is good, how can he allow evil in the world?" When there is a natural disaster like a tornado or earthquake, we find even Christians attributing the event to God's justice. Sometimes, they explain it as God's means of testing our faith. Yet Jesus made it quite clear that there is no connection whatsoever between natural disasters and human sinfulness. When his listeners asked him about a tower in Siloam which fell to the ground and killed eighteen persons, Jesus pointed out that the accident in no way indicated that the victims had been more guilty than anyone else in Jerusalem.

Since the Word of God tells us that everything created is "very good," we cannot really say that anything in nature is evil in itself. What, then, is evil? In Christian tradition, evil has been described as a privation of good. But this notion requires an explanation; "privation of good" is a construct that is very difficult to comprehend. When we say that evil is the absence of good, we are not saying that evil is nothing. Evil is destructive.

In chapter six, we noted that all creatures move toward fuller being. Even on the elemental level, atoms combine to form the more complex unity of a molecule. St. Thomas said created beings "imitate God" in pouring themselves out in the creation of new beings. Evil is the reversal of this tendency toward fuller being. Evil refers to the capacity to diminish being or to destroy it.

We use the phrase "natural evil" to designate a destructive force which cannot be charged to any human agency but arises out of natural factors. When we judge natural events to be evil, our judgment is made in reference to the human suffering that is the consequence of them. What do we mean when we talk about a "greater" evil or a "lesser" evil? Evil itself has no place in the hierarchy of being. So our description cannot mean that one evil is more positive than the other or that one evil has more being than the other. Evil is not a thing. A greater evil, therefore, is the devastation of more beings or higher forms of being. In either case, evil is an enemy of being.

All created beings are created out of nothing. They can advance toward fuller being or they can slip back toward nothingness. Slipping back from the realization of the potentialities for being is a reversal of the creative process. Even though we are assured of the final outcome, we know that there are many tragedies and much "waste" along the way. One way that theologians have tried to deal with the ambiguity that is inherent in creation is by the consideration of the "risk" of creation.

In creation, God gives being, and he gives it to innumerable kinds of particular beings. This makes possible the expression of Being in an almost infinitely diversified community of beings. But the creative process involves risk. In creation, there is a genuine self-giving of Being. God opens himself, so to speak, and pours himself into nothing. He gives it being. In so doing, he takes the risk that his own self-giving will be turned, in the creature, toward destruction rather than toward fuller being. This is the risk that is sometimes called the "weakness" of God.

The vulnerability of God is shown most vividly in the crucified Jesus who places himself at the mercy of the world. And yet, his very weakness is his strength. A God who hoarded all his Being and refused to take the risk of sharing it can hardly be called God. Only when God confers being on others and goes out of himself into creation can we know him as Holy Being. Only when he takes the risk involved in limited beings can we recognize him and worship him as a God of Love. Love, as self-giving and letting-be, is always a risk.

The more such love exposes itself in risk, the more it accomplishes in conferring being (see chapter six—the idea of presence). Even where God appears in weakness, he shows his power in calling beings out of nothing. Our belief in Divine Providence tells us that God's self-giving is steadily overcoming the negative forces of evil by bringing all beings into a greater union with Being. But the risk is real and the cost is dear. In the last analysis, all that we can say is that this tragic element is somehow justified by the inestimable worth of the end.

But the tragic element is not to be interpreted as a fate imposed on us by God. Rather, it is a very real risk that God takes if anything finite is to have being. Natural evil is not an instrument of God's justice; it is not God's way of testing us. Natural evil seems to be more the inevitable "side-effect" in the creation of particular beings. To demand a world in which there would be no natural evil is to demand an unchanging, unmoving universe. In such a universe there can be no growth, no relatedness, no development. We know, for example, that we can never have a pollution-free atmosphere. Even if man were to cease all industrial activity, he would not be able to control the natural accidents such as fire or stop the radiations from space. We tolerate a certain level of pollution only because of some desirable end. The pollution is the undesirable side-effect we risk in working toward the desired goal. To eliminate it, one would be forced to "throw out the baby with the bath water."

Evil is not without its lessons for the human race. In a universe where no one could suffer or get hurt, we are told, we would not develop strength of character or appreciate deep human relations. Without frustration, there is little development of selfhood. One psychiatrist calls this frustration-less world "nature's booby trap." He points out that certain patients are very close to being "impossible cases." These are not God-forsaken waifs. They are intelligent, attractive, affluent adults who experienced very few frustrations while growing up. Everything went their way. Their material needs were always well satisfied. They found easy acceptance among their peers because they were physically attractive. School subjects presented no difficulty. Seldom challenged, nearly never frustrated, they failed to develop the coping mechanisms and inner resources needed in an adult world. When the inevitable confrontation took place, these adults resorted to their infantile patterns of relating to people. When these proved inadequate, they fell apart. Their own "blessings" acted as a shield protecting them from the real world of genuine relationships where give and take are a part of everyday life.

After everything has been said, we still have to admit there are loose ends that we cannot pull together.

Sin and Evil

Evil remains very much a mystery and our efforts to transmute it into a solvable problem can lead only to simplistic solutions. God's words to Job are still relevant: "Who is this that obscures the divine plans with words of ignorance?" We can only concur with Isaiah: "My thoughts are not your thoughts, nor are your ways my ways, says the Lord. As high as the heavens are above the earth, so high are my ways above your ways and my thoughts above your thoughts."

Evil becomes more painfully acute when we arrive at the level of human existence. Once we introduce freedom and responsibility, we are confronted with the reality of sin. Sin is a purely religious term. It includes notions of guilt and wrongdoing, but it is not synonymous with either one of them. Scripture refers to sin as "missing the mark." We talk about "falling" into sin. Such a fall suggests a failure to attain. Missing the mark is a falling short of our authentic possibility. It is a failure to live up to our potential. Sin is a failure to become the kind of human persons God intended us to be when he created us in his image.

The full seriousness of sin cannot be grasped, of course, until we have come to understand what our human potentialities really are. We can arrive at that knowledge only through Christ who showed us in our own flesh what it means to be genuinely human. St. Paul says: "All have sinned and all fall short of the glory of God." None of us is as fully alive and truly human as he might be. We fail to allow Being to express itself in us as freely as Jesus did.

Our failure to let the light of Being shine through our flesh led theologians to speak of the "darkened image" of God. Since we Christians have a tendency to interpret our faith on the objective level, the language about the darkened image came to be thought of as a description of this "thing" called sin. The image of a black spot that tarnished the soul—another "thing"—became standard repertoire. Of course, a mortal sin was so big it enveloped the whole soul! While this might be a slight exaggeration, it does point out the futility of converting religious concepts into concrete objects.

On the same level is the person who evaluates himself according to external rules only. Someone once said that the man who sins, acknowledges it and repents, is in a much better position than a man who has NOT sinned and thinks he has acted rightly! The man who has not sinned measures himself against the commandments and can truthfully say that he has not lied, he has not cheated, he has not lusted. But he says nothing about what he has done that is positive. Has he done anything to improve the quality of life; has he arrived at a new awareness of his relatedness to others; has he been involved in the building of genuine community with others? In other words, has he responded to the call of Being; is he faithful to his vocation?

In popular usage, "sin" usually means some actual act or deed of wrongdoing. Even among Christians, sin is often viewed as a breaking of one of the ten commandments. That such interpretations of sin are inadequate was hinted at in the Gospel. Jesus tried to get his listeners to go beyond the law. He tried to free them for a response-ability that lay beyond the call of duty. He suggested that, even after they had done everything that was expected of them, they still admit they were "useless servants" because they had done no more than their "duty." If sin were simply a matter of obeying rules, this judgment would have been unreasonable.

Sin and Evil

Sound Christian theology has always put the emphasis where it belongs: on the attitude or disposition of the person. The attitude is the fundamental evil because the deeds flow from it. The deed is the outcome or the product of an evil disposition. The outward deed is only a sign that something is wrong "on the inside." Jesus stated quite clearly that nothing on the outside—not even a devil—can contaminate a man. All the evil deeds a man carries out have their source in the center of his being. They issue from his "heart." The real sin dwells inside the sinner.

Sin, the evil disposition, has always been described in traditional Christian theology as a turning away from God toward creatures. Unfortunately, this was often misinterpreted to mean that one should not get too involved with people. Therefore, if the parish priest enjoyed many warm, human relationships and spent much time on "non-religious" activities, he could not, according to this interpretation, be a very "spiritual" man. But turning toward creatures in an evil sense has nothing to do with the time one spends with others. The sin, as we have already noted, is in the disposition.

Sin is the uncaring attitude that allows God, other people, and self to become strangers to us. It is an estrangement from Being. This means that we seek ultimate meaning and fulfillment either in ourselves or others apart from God. Because we do not acknowledge the Being which makes meaning and fulfillment possible at all, we lose sight of our true selves and fail to discern the reality of others. We begin to see them more as objects that are useful or beneficial or useless. We no longer sense our relatedness as persons whose life-giving source is the same Father. We simply "forget Being."

We cannot forget Being and continue to be genuinely human. Spiritual directors have traditionally used the term "worldly" to describe human existence that forgets Being. Worldliness is the basic sin of the world. It is a form of idolatry, as we shall see. To be worldly is to be totally committed to created beings. To be worldly is to understand the meaning of one's life in terms of finite beings apart from God. It means the seeking of ultimate fulfillment in this world. Since creatures now command the loyalty and devotion that properly belong to God, worldliness is idolatry.

Most people probably consider themselves much too modern to revert to idolatry because we tend to associate this evil with the "graven image." Since we Catholics have gotten rid of most of our plastic statues, we may feel that the Church has been purged of idolatry. But idolatry, like any other sin, must reside in the person. Idolatry must signify a certain attitude toward existence. It must be a direction that one allows his life to take.

The people of Old Testament times were not so naive as we sometimes suppose they must have been. They inveighed against idolatry because they perceived that such commitment to created beings stunts personal growth and distorts the whole meaning of human existence. This "sin of the world" inevitably results in dehumanization and depersonalization. John the Baptist said of Jesus: "He is the Lamb of God who takes away the SIN of the world." Jesus is the only human being to whom we can look for ultimate human fulfillment. He can help us overcome worldliness because he is "not of this world." His prayer for us is that we remain in the world while refusing to be merely "of the world."

The world cannot ultimately satisfy us because it,

Sin and Evil

also, is "fallen." This "world" refers to the large-scale perversion of values, the massive disorientation in human society. Since man first introduced sin into the world, the evil has grown in leaps and bounds. Decisions made by one generation pass their evil effects along to the next. Collective standards and patterns of behavior take on a force that irresistibly carries everyone along with it. Even in the world of things, we can find ourselves dragged along as part of the machinery in a direction we do not wish to go. We often hear people talking about the "rat race." This description hardly conveys the idea that it's fun and we want to continue running.

We can't stop the world and get off. We can't turn the clock back and start building humanity all over again in a new mold. We can't erase the slate and begin anew. The sense of helplessness in the face of these conditions which no one seems to be able to control has led to the idea that sin must be something super-human. The destructive power unleashed in the world is often referred to as the "demonic" element in the world. We even have a "Flip Wilson syndrome" which blames it all on the devil. But we cannot blame the human condition on some poor devil. St. Paul explicitly states that it was through man that "sin entered the world."

We are born into a situation that is already oriented in a certain direction, but this still does not take away human freedom. The notion of original sin tries to balance the individual and social orientation toward sin against the idea of personal responsibility. Sometimes Christians get very much upset with God over the idea of original sin. The whole thing seems so unfair. But original sin is not some kind of fate that God imposes on us. Original sin is tied in with the risk of creation. It is part of that tragic element that was discussed in the section on natural evil.

Let us place the notion of original sin within the context of creation. Human existence is not sinful in itself; as part of creation, it is "very good." But human existence is the condition that makes sin possible. Each one of us has his own center of consciousness and interest. Each one of us interprets the world from his own perspective. Since we are not all one whole, but are, rather, a multiplicity of beings, sin becomes possible. The tendency that seems operative from the beginning is that each one of us tries to set up his own personal center as the center of everything. This is true of the group as well as the individual. It reminds one of the anecdote from Abraham Lincoln's life. When someone asked him why his two sons were crying so vigorously, he replied that their problem was the same as that of the rest of the world. Mr. Lincoln had three walnuts, and each son was demanding two of them.

Of ourselves, we are not able to reverse this process. Sin is truly a slavery for the individual and for the whole human race. But this slavery has been brought about by man's voluntary decisions. It is as if there is a critical moment at which the action initiated by man becomes a kind of runaway escalation that drags man along with it whether he wills it or not. It is similar to the critical mass in nuclear physics; once it is exceeded, it sets up a chain reaction that the scientist can no longer control. We can sense the snowballing effect of evil in the present Watergate incident. As Martin Buber observed: "Sin is not an undertaking which man can break off when the situation becomes critical, but a process started by him, the control of which is withdrawn from him at a fixed moment."

Sin and Evil

In spite of all this, man does not cease to be human. He does, however, lose much of his power to fulfill the potentialities of a fully human existence. Yet, the same condition that makes sin possible makes possible a rich diversity in unity. The gift of Being to innumerable particular beings makes possible a community of love and fellowship. Community in diversity far exceeds in richness and beauty any kind of uniformity or unity through sameness. The awareness of the possibility of human community leads man to reach out beyond himself for the Gracious Presence of the Other. As St. Augustine put it: "Our hearts are restless until they rest in Thee."

There is no way that the child who interprets life on the sensual level can grasp the concept of sin. He can learn that adults disapprove of certain actions or language, but he cannot fathom why. Often, we make the mistake of thinking that the child can discern right from wrong when, actually, what he has learned is that certain modes of behavior will be punished. This type of conditioning is a very important preparatory stage to true moral development. However, we can inhibit growth in moral development if we give the child the idea that God punishes every little fault and failing. We know of many instances of children who were terrified of confession, for example, not because they comprehended the heinousness of sin but because they feared God's punishment so much.

The child who can understand concrete logic can master the notion of "sins" but not sin itself. He can learn about rules and check his conduct against external standards. Again, there is nothing wrong with this way of dealing with sin at this level because this is the most the child is capable of grasping at this stage. He interprets life very objectively. He needs external standards to live by. Psychologists frequently point out the problems created by parents who fail to establish definite rules and then punish as though those rules had been established in the child's mind.

This is not to say that the child will not rebel against the rule; but his rebellion does not make the rule superfluous. He needs to learn limits just the way adults do. His rebellion is a sign that he is maturing and has to be given an opportunity to view the rule in the light of his new understanding. Young adolescents are ambivalent about rules. For example, in a discussion about the disciplinary measures used by their own parents, a group of adults discovered a certain commonality. The matter that came up for discussion was: Did your parents set a definite time for you to be home in the evening? Those who had no rules agreed that they would have argued with their parents over the rule—as did the "ruled" group. But the non-ruled group also agreed that they had felt at that time that their parents did not really care about them very much since they had not bothered to set any standard for them to follow. In fact, some of the non-ruled admitted they used to pretend that their parents had actually set a time limit for them.

What we as adults forget is that young people do not always want to go along with the crowd. Since they are not yet strong enough in their own convictions to withstand peer group pressure, they sometimes welcome the opportunity to "blame it on their parents." Parental guidance is a source of support for them when they can say, "I would go along, but you know how my parents are! I don't want to have a hassle with them."

When the student is ready for an interpretation of

sin on the spiritual level, it is a waste of time to continue repeating the explanations he learned at an earlier stage of growth. To speak to him only of rule-keeping and duty at a time when he is opening up to the Spirit is to deprive him of a more meaningful existence. When one has been challenged by the Spirit and discovers a deeper relationship with Christ, he learns to follow the rule of love which far surpasses any external regulation. Now there are no limits to the demands he allows Christ to make. When he fails, he feels miserable not because he fears punishment or because a rule has been broken, but because he has been unfaithful to Love.

DOCUMENTATION

From the very dawn of history, man misused his liberty to set himself against God and seek fulfillment apart from his Creator. In this matter, man has not made much progress. If we honestly search our hearts, we find the same inclinations. As we look around us, we see an evil that could not have been created by a good God. Because man has disrupted his proper relationship with God right from the beginning, he has become at odds with himself, with others, and with all created things. (GS 13; RE/BT 16)

Man is split within himself. As a result, all of human life, individual and collective, feels the tension between good and evil, light and darkness. He is held as if in chains. In order to free and strengthen man, to renew him inwardly so that he might overcome evil, the Son of God became man. For sin had diminished man's being, thus blocking his path to fulfillment.

The conditions of history and of life are not to be considered the main impediment to human freedom. When we begin to walk the way of salvation, we find that the greatest obstacle is sin. We find that we all fail in love of God. Knowingly and deliberately, we may violate moral values. Religious educators must not be silent about the reality of sin or the gravity of sin. Though the power of sin is great, however, the power of grace is greater. The love of God continually calls the sinner and draws him back to unity with his Father. (GCD 62)

The crucial test for religious education will be a proper balance between the awareness of sin and the message of hope. Religious education must reflect the Gospel's realistic view of the human condition which recognizes the fact of evil and personal sin while affirming hope. The Gospel proclaims the dignity and freedom of each person. The message of Christ gives us the assurance that all men have a right to hope for personal salvation with its conquest of isolation, injustice, sin and death. (TT 8)

PART THREE

COMMUNITY

The religious community preserves the spirit of a religion and enables that religion to function as an organized force in the lives of men. The modern idea that religion is merely a personal matter is highly misleading. Even Jesus was dependent upon his religious community for his original beliefs and attitudes. He was nourished by its traditions long before he challenged them or sought to imbue them with a new vision. An individual may reject membership in a religious community, but he does not therewith embrace a purely personal religion. He will continue to be influenced by the beliefs and practices of some religious community. Even when he rejects certain beliefs, he is rejecting the interpretation he has learned from some religious group.

8. Worship and Prayer

Worship is at the heart of every religion. When an outsider wants to find out what it is like to be a member of a particular religious community, he observes them at worship. Worship is the most obvious outward expression of a religion. How the members of a religion view God, man, and the world will be reflected in their worship. Yet many people today question the relevance of worship. Even adult Catholics ask: "Why do I have to go to Mass on Sunday?", "Why do I have to confess my sins to a priest when I can confess them directly to God?", "Why can't two people live together without first performing a marriage rite?" All these questions, the Mass and the sacraments, are established forms of worship in the Catholic religion.

But what is worship? Worship is described as a cult. The word, cult, comes from the Latin word meaning CARE. Care includes feeling, valuing, and acting; it is always intentional. The idea of caring is brought out in the closely related term, cultivate. To cultivate is to prepare the soil for the growth of new life. Cultivation involves loosening and breaking up the hard soil so the seed has room to breathe. The purpose of worship is to lead to growth in the Spirit. Worship is a way of cultivating a deeper understanding of Holy Being and a more profound sharing in that Being. Scripture warns us not to "harden our hearts." To experience new life, we must allow enough "room" for the Spirit to breathe where he will.

It is said that man is a being who cares about being. He questions his own existence. He wants to know who he is and what he is all about. Religious man goes further. He cares about Being as well. He wants to know his Creator. He wants to be united in some way with his God. He yearns to see the "Face of God." His response to the Holy, the way he expresses his devotion to this God he has come to know, is his worship. When there is no one to respond to Being, when there is no one who cares, Yahweh's complaint to Jeremiah is made concrete again. "The land becomes desolate—the rich land, a desert—because no one takes it to heart."

Worship takes place within the context of community. Sometimes Catholics argue that they, as individuals, ought to be allowed to worship "as they please." But there is no such thing as an individual form of worship. An individual may follow his unique form of spirituality, but that is not a new form of worship. In fact, his spirituality is most likely derived from his experience of community worship. This is not to say, however, that he cannot worship as an individual within a worshiping community. He can and must.

Man is a social being and all aspects of his spiritual life are affected by the culture of his religious group. The community itself is the natural result of the tendency we have as human beings to express our inner experiences in outward acts and to share our religious experience with others who acknowledge the same reality. Long before we learn to think for ourselves, we are deeply influenced by the ideas and practices of our religious community. Apart from that community, Jesus pointed out, we are like a branch cut off from the vine. It "withers and dies."

Worship and Prayer 113

Worship is not some kind of burden that God places upon us. We take that position only when we take a one-sided view of worship. We think of what we are doing for God and forget what God is doing for us. True worship is a happening in which God comes to man. God is the one who takes the initiative. It is God who invites: "You shall be my people; I will be your God." It is Christ who beckons: "Do this in memory of me." It is God who draws near to us and addresses us: "Everything is ready; come to the feast."

Members of a religious community come together to worship, not because God needs it but because religious man needs it. When we think of worship only in terms of duty or obligation, it can lead to distortions in the Christian concept of God. God is not going to sit on some lonely throne and sulk on Sunday because Catholics do not go to Mass. He is not going to figure out ways to punish us for breaking the Church law. But what does happen is that we who call ourselves Christians or Catholics and do not join the community in worship become an underprivileged class. We lead lives of deprivation. We choose to live in a spiritual ghetto. We isolate ourselves and cut ourselves off from countless opportunities to enrich our own lives and experience deeper joys.

Since worship is continuous with life, we can learn something about the meaning of worship if we focus attention on those aspects of ordinary human behavior that parallel our conduct at worship. If we reflect upon the way that human beings relate to persons, places, and things, we soon discover that man has a basic need for symbolization. It goes on all the time even though we may be unaware of it. We human beings have a need to give overt expression to our experience and ideas. We express our inner being through symbolic activities. Because of this basic need to go outside ourselves and give expression to our inner experience, man has developed myth and ritual, art and science.

One symbolic activity is so universal and so characteristic of man it sets man apart from the animal. This activity is the use of human language. The common human symbol, the mark of humanity, is the word. God himself chose this symbol for his own self-expression. It is through the word that God goes out of himself to man. It is through the word that man, made in the image of God, reaches out to his neighbor.

Speech is fundamental in human communication. We know the frustrations of a child who cannot say what he experiences. Young Helen Keller, unable to move outside her silent world to give expression to her inner being, could only react at times in violent outbursts. She could laugh and cry, but she could not talk. We cry as adults when an inner experience is too profound to put into words. When we are shaken to our roots and our bodies can no longer contain our experience, we cry. That is why we cry when we are extremely sad or extremely joyous. Both are experiences we cannot SAY.

Because the word is so essential, Moses asked God to SAY who he is. We do the same thing in worship. We ask God to say who he is. And we listen to the way he expresses himself in his Word. We, in turn, try to put into words our experience of God which begins with his Word. Christians experience a human need to say in words all that has been revealed. In fact, Jesus demands it. After the apostles had accompanied Jesus over a period of time, Jesus expected them to be able to say who he was. He asked them through Peter: "Who do you SAY that I am?"

To state that we do not need worship is to say that we, as a religious community, do not have to be human. For if we did not try to put into words our inner experience of God, we would be frustrated in our humanity. To be denied the opportunity of expressing our experience of Being-in-Love and sharing it with others would be tragic. In fact, the more we come together, the greater becomes the need to continue speaking in worship. As the divine Word permeates our being, we have a more intense desire to express it. As Jeremiah puts it: "I say to myself, I will not mention him, I will speak in his name no more. But then it becomes like a fire burning in my heart, imprisoned in my bones; I grow weary holding it in, I cannot endure it."

But just saying our experience is not enough. We are embodied beings, and our bodies cannot be separated from our spiritual experience. Our bodies are not just food-getting instruments. We move and act and perform. We use our bodies as a means of expressing our persons. An infant makes all kinds of motions, but only gradually does he learn that certain bodily movements convey particular messages. When he grasps this notion, he has learned "body language," so to speak. He has learned not motions but gestures. Gestures are motions that express our inner being. When gestures fail to express our true disposition, they revert to the level of empty motion.

When certain gestures are to be repeated again and again, a particular pattern evolves. We call this paradigm of behavior a rite or ritual. Ritual may include all kinds of activities: sitting, standing, singing, washing, eating, speaking. Ritual is not something that is imposed on man; he performs ritual almost instinctively. Ritual must be performed, not because we hope to get something out of it but because we have a sheer inner need to act out our inner experience. We know how frustrated lovers feel when they are unable to act out the love they have for each other. We also know how empty is the sexual performance of such a lover when he acts only to get something out of it rather than allowing it to be an expression of his own inner being. Ritual is never the performance of an act whose end is some material or physical reward.

Let us look at the way a ritual develops in the home. Let us suppose a husband and wife have found that Sunday is a day that differs from other days because of certain meaningful activities the family enjoys together on that day. Because they find these activities enriching, they expect the children to participate in them. Week after week, they follow the same routine. Once the meaningful ritual has been established, it is no longer merely a spontaneous expression of feeling. It becomes a complex, permanent attitude. The pattern cannot be changed by whim without introducing chaos into the household. Only a more meaningful ritual can effect a real change. This usually happens as the nature of the relationship between parents and children changes as the children mature.

The same process occurs in the performance of sacred ritual. When an adult is received into the Church, the Mass may be purely self-expressive. The liturgy allows this new believer to give expression to his feelings and emotions. Participation in the sacramental life is a satisfying experience even on the level of feelings. As the ritual becomes habitual, it no longer serves the purpose of relieving one's feelings. Ritual then assumes a symbolic character meant to demonstrate a personal disposition. It is no longer compulsive self-expression. Now the gestures and words of the ritual express our emotions in a logical rather than a physiological sense. This means that they are symbols of our emotions. They are signs of our inner, complex, permanent attitude. Rites regularly performed, then, are not merely free expressions of feelings but are a "disciplined rehearsal of the right attitudes" (S. Langer).

Once we understand ritual in this way, we can see that the words and gestures of the Mass do not have to be the direct expression of our immediate personal feelings. What is demanded is that we have the desire to assume the attitude that is being demonstrated in the performance of the ritual. So we kneel when we do not feel like kneeling to demonstrate our attitude of genuine submission and dedication to the God whom we have come to know through Christ. We stand when we do not feel like standing because we want to have an attentive and respectful attitude toward the Word of God. When we sit, it is not merely to relax. Rather, we assume that position because we want to develop an attitude of careful listening and reflection upon the Word and deeds of God. If our feelings happen to correspond with the attitude being demonstrated, the liturgy will undoubtedly be more satisfying emotionally. But we should not expect that to happen each time we participate in the liturgy.

Ritual activity is always performed for the group; it is never done merely for an isolated individual. Rites demonstrate the fundamental dispositions that should govern the everyday life of all members. This is why ritual builds up a unity within the group. It transforms the collectivity into genuine community. For Catholics, the ritual most clearly a sign of unity is the Eucharist. In the formalized gestures and words of the Eucharistic liturgy, Catholics recognize the attitude that must be theirs because it is the attitude of Christ. They recognize this only in the formalized ritual that the community has performed for centuries. Because of the Reality revealed to us in the Liturgy of the Eucharist, we would not allow the priest to change the words of consecration, for example, into a mere expression of his own personal emotional state. Nor would we allow him to use different objects in the performance of the ritual.

Ritual then helps us to develop the proper attitude toward Being. To say that we do not want to worship is to say that we do not want to learn what kind of attitude we ought to have before God. It is to say that we do not want to grow in Being. We are then very much like St. Augustine who, when he became aware of the call of Being, protested: "Not yet, Lord, not yet!" St. Augustine knew that once he opened himself to the Spirit, he could never be the same again. He knew that a new awareness of God's presence would bring with it a more critical self-judgment. If he lapsed into old habits, he would feel a guilt he had not felt before. He would have to assume a new attitude toward himself and others. Jesus made this clear when he said: "If I had not come to them and spoken to them, they would not be guilty of sin; now, however, their sin cannot be excused." The presence of Holy Being is always a blend of grace and judgment at the same time.

Through our worship ritual God touches us in a way that cannot be equalled by any other experience. The rites dramatize certain events in such a way that they bring order and continuity into our lives. The past event is re-presented, made present, even as we anticipate its fulfillment in the future. In this, the movement in worship is analogous to the development of the person. The events in our personal past history which impressed us have made us what we are today; yet we are not yet what we shall be. The present, acting self remembers its past while it anticipates its own future. To forget any one of these dimensions of our temporality is to stunt our growth. Without remembrance and anticipation, we cannot celebrate life. Our celebrations of birthdays and anniversaries are made possible by our own temporality.

Because of the rich meaning—remembered and anticipated—in its symbols and ritual, the liturgy is performed week after week. Liturgy means the "work of the people" and yet we call it a celebration. We celebrate the Mass and we celebrate the sacraments. What do we mean when we use this language? We have already seen that ritual is not the spontaneous airing of our feelings or emotions. So our worship celebration is not like the spontaneous cheering of football fans for their triumphant team. Neither does a sacred celebration have anything in common with party fun. Even etymologically, celebration and party are worlds apart.

Celebration refers to special public performances. It means frequenting or associating with often and habitually. Celebration and fame are closely related. Fame depends on reporting, speaking, saying what one stands for or having others say what they think one stands for. The famous person is a celebrity. Our worship celebration, then, is an acting out of who we say we are. Our fame in society is connected to the way we celebrate and what we celebrate. Celebration is not a one-time performance; it is a continuing process. If we are genuinely celebrating the Eucharist or the other sacraments, our lives must show its effects. For the early Christians this must have been true to a very high degree. They gained fame in the wider community because of their lived fellowship with others, a disposition that is rehearsed in the celebration of the Eucharist.

We know that our Eucharistic celebration is both a meal and a sacrifice. In the past, the sacrifice dimension was emphasized so much that the meal aspect was almost forgotten. Today, many have gone to the opposite extreme and insist that the Mass is a meal. But the meal aspect does not suddenly replace the sacrificial dimension. So, to explain to children that the Mass is a meal is not adequate. A meal in itself is not sacred; it must be made sacred. The word, sacrifice, is made up of two Latin words meaning "to make sacred." Any object or event can become sacred to religious man. It is his attitude that transmutes the ordinary into the sacred. This does not mean that religious people run around looking for objects or events they can call sacred. Rather, the sacred is revealed to those who are in a disposition to receive the deeper reality that lies below the surface.

What singles out the sacred is the Being that appears through the finite symbol or event. The man of faith does not see an objective reality that is different from that which the unbeliever sees. But, because he goes far below the surface, the religious man perceives a depth of being that is so rich it cannot be captured by ordinary concepts. Once the sacred is perceived, it impels man to move outside himself toward others. That is why religious communities inevitably grow out of such an experience of Holy Being.

So a Catholic who says he does not need the Mass because he "finds God in another person" must be able, as pointed out by Father Borchertmeyer, to validate that experience on two counts. First, he must be able to

Worship and Prayer

say that he is disposed to perceive and accept Being as it reveals itself to him in the other person. Second, both parties must be moved by their experience to reach outward to others. If, on the contrary, they get all tied up in each other and forget the rest of the world, it is more likely that they are finding need-satisfaction on a profane level. One cannot experience God without becoming more aware of one's relatedness to others outside one's chosen circle.

This going out of oneself is an element in the act of making sacred. Separation from what we hold dear on an ordinary plane is what constitutes the sacrificial aspect in worship. Sacrifice throughout the history of religions has meant either gifts or communion rites. Sacrifice, the act of making sacred, was always an attempt to be united with the Holy—especially after such union had been disrupted by sin. The union with the sacred was symbolized by the sacred meal. But the sacred meal never consisted in merely taking food.

Giving has always been intimately connected with the sacred meal. The offering is one characteristic which all sacrifices have in common. To give is to place oneself in relation to the other. Communion itself requires this notion of giving or offering. A man and wife who do not offer anything of themselves to each other throughout the day will hardly achieve intense personal union with each other during moments of sexual intimacy. So if we do not offer ourselves to God during the week, it is hardly likely that our Sunday offering can be intensely personal.

When the bread and wine are offered, they are set apart from ordinary usage to serve a special function. In the very act of being offered, they are made sacred. They become the sacrifice of Christ. When we speak of the sacrifice of Christ only in terms of bloody or unbloody victims, we focus on an aspect of sacrifice that is offensive to modern ears. We must remember that any symbol that offends our sensibilities loses its symbolic value. God never demanded an innocent victim as payment for sin. Even in the Old Testament, prophets inveighed against this idea. As Hosea put it: "It is mercy that I desire, not sacrificial victims and knowledge of God rather than holocausts." That God "neither desires nor delights in sacrifices and holocausts" was again emphasized in Hebrews. Jesus replaced the ancient idea of sacrifice with the notion of obedience. His prayer, "I have come to do your will, O God," expresses a disposition most appropriate in worship. The sacrifice of Christ in terms of his obedience was described in chapter two.

Just as a religious community seeks outward expression in worship, so religious man expresses his religious belief through prayer. Public worship and private prayer are interrelated. If those who participate in public worship do not engage in prayer when they are alone, it is difficult to see how that worship can be anything but cold and formal. Private prayer and public worship follow the same patterns with respect to purpose and content. Just as the movements of worship move from penance and praise to offering and communion, so also private prayer must lead to a spirit of obedience or submission in order to arrive at communion with God. In Christian spirituality, the unitive way has always been considered the summit of one's prayer life.

The spirit of prayer is not the same as the activity of saying prayers. However, one cannot develop a Christian spirit of prayer until he has first learned or heard the formal prayers of the Christian community. The normal way to learn any language, including the language of prayer, is to become habituated to its unformulated rules through the use of the language. One cannot be creative and spontaneous with the skills of the language unless he has first learned proper use of those skills. Along with the other elements of ritual, the established prayers of the Church help us to assume the right attitude toward God, our neighbor, and the world.

If we examine more closely the language we use in the common prayers of the Church, we may come to understand the function of these prayers in the development of a mature religious personality. Let us take as an example a prayer with which most Christians are familiar, the Our Father. Christ taught us this prayer so that we might use it as a model for developing Christian attitudes. What are those attitudes? First, notice that there are three movements in the prayer. All three deal with relations: to God, to ourselves and our neighbor, to the world. We address our God familiarly not so much as a daddy who gives us all kinds of things but as a Father who gives life and wills that all should live. It seems that the major concern of the mature Christian must be that all men begin to respond to the call of Being. When we ask that God's will be done, we are saying that we want all men to be obedient, that they all learn how to "hear toward" the Spirit (chapter 3). Of course, if we really mean that, we must be willing to cooperate in Christ's work of building up the Kingdom of God. The kingdom theme will be treated in a later chapter since it is so charged with meaning that it demands more detailed discussion.

In the second movement of this great prayer, Christ teaches us that our relatedness to others is on the same level as our daily sustenance. Forgiving others and being reunited with them are just as important as getting enough to eat. One keeps us alive on the physical level; the other keeps us alive on the social level. Once again, we see the importance of both the individual and the communal aspects of human existence. A heart filled with resentments and grievances can only choke any seed of God's Word that is planted in its soil. Such an attitude diminishes Being as it destroys human relatedness.

In the final movement, Christ warns us how easily we can be caught up in the activities and pursuits of the "world." This world is the one identified by St. John as that which is opposed to the sacred. It is the world which hates Christ. It is the world that forgets Being. We are taught by this prayer to ask our loving Father for his support and strength in resisting the seductive call of this world which can lead only to a fruitless search for happiness in created beings apart from their Creator. The great temptation of this world is that of idolatry (see chapter 7).

Jesus not only talked about prayer, he also lived a life of prayer. He does not disparage the activity of saying prayers. He says it is all right to ask the Father to satisfy our needs, provided we keep a proper perspective. Jesus says: "Ask and you shall receive, seek and you shall find, knock and it shall be opened to you." But he also warns us not to pray "like the pagans." We must not think that our words have some kind of magical power over God. We must not think that praying with more words is better than praying with few words. Jesus tells us to focus not on the needs but on the One who can satisfy those needs. He tells us not to be perpetually worried about things because we have a Father

Worship and Prayer

who is aware of our real needs. A believer, Jesus tells us, is more concerned with the needs of the kingdom.

Are these prayers really answered? The author of the letter to the Hebrews tells us something about the attitude we must assume if our prayers are to be fruitful. This epistle states explicitly that Jesus was heard "because of his reverence." But what does it mean to be reverent in prayer? Reverence is one of those words whose meaning transcends the concrete definition. It always infers more than is visible. In fact, the Greek word from which it comes means "to see," meaning that the reverent person sees something that is not immediately obvious. Because the reverent person sees beyond the superficial, he is attentive, careful, watchful —lest he miss the deeper reality. When Jesus asked his apostles to join him in prayer in the garden, he invited them to "watch" one hour with him. He was asking them to stay awake and be alert to the promptings of the Spirit. He was asking them to be reverent. The person who reveres Being centers his attention and activities on Being. He is devoted to and honors Being from motives that are as impelling as a vow.

Only the truly reverent person can pray genuine prayers of supplication. The suppliant remains supple in the presence of Being which, in reverence, he perceives. To be supple means literally "to be capable of being bent, or folded without creases, cracks, or breaks." Jesus and his mother have much to teach us about reverence and supplication. Their prayers during moments of very difficult personal decisions can serve as a model for those of us who wish to grow in the spirit of prayer.

When Mary is not certain about the way she is to carry out God's plan, she asks, "How shall this be . . . ?" As soon as she comes to see that the Spirit of God is directing the course of her life, she says simply, "Let it be. . . ." She is supple enough to make adjustments in her life. She focuses her attention on Being. She is not overwhelmed by worries about what people might say. Similarly, Jesus in the garden is faced with a very difficult personal decision. To remain true to the call of Being, as he perceives it, means inevitable conflict with those in authority. Being truly humble in prayer, Jesus makes no undue claims. He is not presumptuous, assertive, or aggressive. He simply asks if there is any way out, if there is any way of circumventing the hateful destruction that is bearing down on him. Jesus, the suppliant, is not broken by the pressure of it all. Ever watchful, always attentive to Being, Jesus focuses on the true Center. He prays only that he be faithful to his vocation ". . . may your will be done."

Mary and Jesus could pray as true suppliants because they lived a life of prayer. Since Jesus tells us to "pray always," prayer cannot be simply a matter of saying prayers. At some point in our spiritual life, conversation with God about our activities and needs must be superseded by the sense of intimate union with God. The insecure lover focuses on himself and what he does for his beloved. He measures the response by what is done for him in return. While more mature lovers do things for each other, the deeper meaning of their personal union is at the heart of all they do.

An incident in the life of Jesus may help us gain the proper perspective in prayer. Although this account has been interpreted as being symbolic of the active and contemplative religious orders, it is just as truly a description of the prayer life of the individual. In a brief passage in the Gospel, we are told about a visit Jesus

Worship and Prayer

made at the home of two friends, Martha and Mary. Martha was very busily engaged in doing things for Jesus. She wanted to please him and was concentrating on what she was doing. Mary preferred to enjoy the presence of Jesus. Because she reverenced his person, she was attentive to his Word. She was attuned to the mystery of Jesus' person and was careful not to miss the deeper reality being revealed to her. Martha, being more pragmatic, felt that Mary would be more productive if she would involve herself in Martha's activity.

Jesus then points out the necessity of centering our activity around that which can impart some meaning to it. Jesus does not condemn Martha. He just reminds her that there is more to one's spiritual life than the things we do or would like to do for the Lord. Mary's obedience, her "hearing toward" Jesus, is the "better part" of one's life of prayer. So Martha and Mary might be considered as symbols of our own attitudes or disposition. Martha is the symbol of a mind that is busy working out the details of everyday life. Having worked them out, we run to the Lord for help in carrying out our plans. But the focus is still our own activity. Mary is the symbol of a mind that heeds the command of Christ, "Peace, be still." When we learn how to calm the turbulence in our minds, we create a stillness that can more easily perceive the gentle murmur of the Spirit. We create an atmosphere of receptivity for the Word. This symbolic stillness is emphasized in the Church's Christmas liturgy when we are reminded that it was in the "stillness of the night" that the almighty Word entered our world.

What can children learn about worship and prayer? The child at the sensual level needs the kinds of prayers that reassure him. He needs to feel comfortable and safe with God. He can learn to acknowledge God in all the beautiful things and happy experiences in his life. Since the child is deeply influenced by the attitudes of his parents, it may be necessary to involve the parents in discussions about prayer and worship. An adult who has not developed a deep sense of Christian prayer cannot foster such growth in the child. A parent or teacher who goes to Mass on Sunday only because it is a law is unlikely to convey the idea that worship is indispensable because it fulfills a basic human need.

Children on the objective level resemble pragmatic Martha. They are very much taken up with their own concrete activities and problems. Psychologists tell us that children at this stage enjoy testing their powers of memory. If this is true, it would seem that students ought to be given opportunities at this stage of their development to memorize basic creedal formulas and common prayers. It is not necessary that they master the meaning of every phrase any more than they do when they learn how to recite the Pledge of Allegiance to our country. A simple explanation in their own language should serve as initiation into the proper Christian attitudes to assume in prayer.

While duty or law may have been a motivating force in the past, it is no longer effective in moving people to pray or worship. Students capable of interpreting life on a spiritual plane are neither inspired nor challenged by reminders of Sunday obligations. Often, stressing Church law is the easy way out. When a student asks us why he should pray or join the community for worship, he is asking a question that has no easy answer. "Because the Church says so" merely places the question in another context. It does not tell us why the Church herself needs prayer and worship. Religious education has failed when adults have no more profound reason for worshiping than that of obeying a law. These adults have a right to express their grievances at having been denied a more meaningful life of worship and prayer.

DOCUMENTATION

As members of a believing community, we are called to participate in worship. Reflection upon God's goodness renews our hope and should prompt us to give open expression to this hope especially in the liturgy. In the liturgy, we offer ourselves and all our activity to God so that we might receive in return the words of life and the grace to profess the truth in love. This truth must shine through all our actions. Our fidelity to the Word of God will show itself by the depth and richness of our human existence. We must increase the "talents" we have been given. (RE/BT Introduction; GCD 48)

By coming together to worship, the members of a parish are enabled to grow in fellowship. This is so because the liturgy is a way of forming not only the individual but also the community. The Eucharist has always been considered a source and symbol of unity among Christians. Through worship and prayer, Christians render as important a service in the building up of community as they do when directly participating in movements for social reform. (TT 25, 29; RE/BT Introduction)

The liturgy is the sacred action of Christ who works through his Church. But the effects of the Mass, the Church's greatest prayer, are not automatic. The more mature a community of faith, the more it lives its worship in spirit and in truth. Since mature faith is essential, religious educators must do more than explain ceremonies. Catechists must promote active, conscious, and willing participation in worship. They can do this in part by helping the students to see the place of prayer, repentance, creed, and community in the life of a mature Christian. All of these are indispensable in the way of salvation. (TT 25)

Christians are called to join with their fellow believers in worship. But the Christian must pray when he is alone, also. Christ challenges him to "pray always" and to "pray to the Father in secret." Private prayer is essential to growth in the spiritual life. Growth in faith is not evolutionary, it must be asked for in prayer. (GCD 25)

There is more to prayer than memorized formulas; however, people cannot pray together as a community unless they share some common prayers. Christians have a rich tradition of prayer from which they can draw for their personal devotions. Students should be familiar with the common prayers of the Church: Sign of the Cross, Our Father, Hail Mary, Apostles' Creed. These prayers have much to teach Christians about their personal prayer. (RE/BT Introduction)

Informal prayer includes not only the spontaneous and familiar conversation with God but also listening and responding to the Spirit. Private prayer and devotions that harmonize with the liturgical seasons can enrich one's spiritual life. Learning to express praise and thanksgiving brings balance into one's prayer life which might otherwise lean toward prayer only in times of difficulty or stress. The aim of prayer and instruction in prayer must be to lead the individual to a life of meditation, contemplation, or union with God. (SC 12, 13)

9. The Sacramental Life

A few years ago, a teacher wrote about her experiences in an inner-city high school. One incident she recalled had to do with a suggestion box she had placed in the classroom. Students were invited to write their opinions, comments, and criticisms and deposit these in the box. One day, the teacher found a note written by a lonely boy. It read, "Happy birthday to me!" As human beings, we do not want all our days to be the same. We want the important events in our lives to stand out with special significance. But unless other persons acknowledge the event, we feel diminished as persons.

A sense of community with others gives us a feeling of worth and importance. The community helps us to discover our own reality and meaning. This sense of belonging will remain a spiritual necessity as long as we wish to continue as individuals and maintain our individuality as adults. In order to give the private events in our lives a public significance, we human beings devise rituals. These celebrations incorporate us more deeply into the life of the community and expand the horizons of our being. Public celebration of a personal experience makes it more real and more meaningful. The celebration of the ritual separates the event from other routine happenings.

Not all the events in our lives are equally important. But there are some human events that have always been judged by man to be significant. These events seem to be rooted in man's fascination with the life-giving forces at work in the world. Man is a creature who is invited to participate in the creation of the world. He is moved to celebrate all forms of creativity. Creation has to do with beginnings, and beginnings are always mysterious. When we begin something, we bring into the world something new, something that was never there before. Each time we begin, we start out in a new direction with fresh ideas and new attitudes. Because we recognize the mystery of beginnings, we set the creative event apart to show it is not a mere repetition of what has gone before. We celebrate the birth of a child. We celebrate the beginning of life together in marriage. We celebrate the passage to life after death.

But life-giving creativity cannot be carried out in isolation. Often, the creative process is reversed by our self-interest. Creation can be sustained only by union and reconciliation. We know that we find new life when we can identify with a unified group. So we celebrate unions and reunions. Those who cherish their shared experiences come together to renew the bonds of unity and friendship. When we have broken ties with someone we love, our spirits sag. We have less life. We don't feel like doing anything. So we have rituals we act out as an outward expression of our desire to be reunited. We apologize, we forgive, we kiss and make up. Then we can begin again with renewed energy and purpose.

A man of faith seeks an ultimate purpose. He wants the important events in his life to assume a religious significance. He knows that life is complete when it is whole, so he seeks a way to fit the events of his life into the total picture revealed by God. So the Church

The Sacramental Life

has designed special rituals to celebrate our Christian beginnings, our unions, and our reunions. The Church blesses our beginnings and offers to support us along the way. It provides occasions when Jesus can touch us individually and unite us more profoundly with his Body.

As the Body of Christ, the Church continues to perform the saving deeds of Jesus. In the community of faith, Christ speaks to us, touches us, heals us, and blesses us. He does this each day in sacramental signs. Each time the priest acts out in word and symbolic gesture the saving event, Christ himself is acting to save us. Salvation (see chapter 6) is the process by which we are made holy. To be made holy is to be made whole. Each time Christ touches us, he imbues our lives with meaning, purpose, and direction. He is already doing for us those things we shall experience in his kingdom.

In the sacraments Christ confronts us with the ultimate fulfillment promised in the kingdom. The sacraments make it possible for us to share in the hope of the final destiny of all mankind. We know that we are destined for perfect community with God and man. The sacraments place our lives in that context of the future and give us the power to work for that community in the present. Christ gives us the strength of his Spirit to oppose the disintegrating influences in our lives. The Spirit moves us to greater unity with others. He acts in us to overcome misery, selfishness, and all that alienates man from his destiny of eternal joy.

In each sacrament, the Spirit comes with gifts of faith, hope, and love. But these gifts are not things we possess once for all. When we say that the Spirit gives us these gifts, we are saying that he establishes a special relationship with Christ which is expressed in faith, hope, and love. The Spirit disposes our hearts to reflect these dimensions of the relationship in our daily lives. This, of course, will not happen automatically. If we do not continue to respond to Christ, faith is lessened. If we lose sight of God's promises, hope is diminished. When we reject communion with others, love is absent.

Faith, hope, and love are not different graces. There is only one grace—the presence of the Holy Spirit. All of us together are given one Spirit. "There is one baptism, one Spirit, one Lord and Savior, Jesus Christ. . . ." That is why we have to exercise caution when we speak of actual graces and sanctifying grace. These are not separate items. Grace has to do with personal intimacy with God; it has nothing to do with the acquisition of a quantity of some mysterious substance. To grow in grace is to grow in God's own kind of being. It is to become more attuned to his Spirit, to become more intensely aware of his presence. If Trinity is Being-in-Love, growing in grace must show itself in an ever-expanding unity with others.

We have a tendency to think of grace as a gift God gives to us in a one-sided fashion. All one has to do is go to the sacraments to get it. It provides security without demands. But grace is not something we receive passively. It is a relationship that is both a task and a challenge. In each sacramental encounter, Christ brings the power of the future into our present and creates new possibilities for existence. Just as he exhibited in his life the integrity and perfection that awaits us in the Kingdom of God, so also he offers us in the sacraments the power to live in the present the way we shall live in eternity.

We do not become like Christ overnight. Often, we prefer to settle at a lower level of meaning by forgetting

The Sacramental Life

who we are called to be. Many times our own immediate interests get in the way. Sometimes we make decisions that contradict the meaning of Christian. We choose to ignore Christ in our dealings with others. That is why we have to keep coming back to the source of our faith, our hope, and our love.

Sacraments are, first of all, acts of faith. In faith, we make the decision to accept the word of Christ and live our lives in accordance with it. If faith is our response to the God who draws near, we have to think about what he has revealed. We have to reflect on the invitation he offers us in each sacrament. We remain responsible before God for our belief. We remain responsible for the way we adhere to him. We have to be convinced that what the sacrament offers is a richer, more responsible way to live. We should know how the sacrament will perfect our relationship with others and the world at large.

The experience of the Spirit is never a wholly inward experience. The Holy Spirit always directs us outward to greater unity with the rest of creation. True faith always leads to genuine selfhood and community. True faith always enables us to make more and more sense of life in the world. It always frees us for response-ability and obedience (see chapter 3). It brings our relationship with Christ to bear in all our important personal decisions. It frees us from the tyranny of things. Faith sheds light on our human possibilities. Each sacrament carries with it the obligation to deepen our understanding of what faith involves. Each sacrament carries with it the charge to strengthen our commitment to Christ.

We cannot use Christ as a substitute for God. Regardless of how rewarding the experience, we can never be content to know that Christ has touched us. Christ never tried to attract people to himself alone. He always made an effort to lead them to the Father. He never claimed to have finished the work of salvation. He promised us his Spirit to carry on what he had begun. Our sacraments are centered in a Triune God. That is why the "Jesus and I" attitude is an inadequate frame of reference for our sacramental lives. It is always to the Father, through Christ, in the Spirit.

Since it is through Christ that we go to the Father, our meeting with him in the sacraments is a source of hope. In hope, we are willing to rely on Christ and his word. When we hope in him, he brings us the power of the future; he gives us the power to create a better tomorrow. When we hope in Christ, we allow him to draw near and heal our isolation. Hope enables us to enter into communion with him. When we hope, we place the meaning of our lives in his hands and trust that he can do only good for us all the days of our lives. To refuse to hope is to render him powerless to help us, just as lack of hope drove Judas away from Jesus.

What we hope for, though, is not some particular good, some particular virtue or grace which we think will enhance our personality or our lives. Christian hope is never merely a matter of hoping for something we want and hope to get. Like faith, hope is an interpersonal relationship. We do not merely believe Jesus, we believe in him. So we do not merely hope, we hope in Christ. What we hope for is not some thing, but our very being and growth as persons. We hope in Christ for our salvation. We hope in him because his vision gives meaning to our lives. We hope in Christ because he helps us to realize our destiny as persons.

When we really hope in Christ, we are freed from bondage to our past and from fear of the future. Such

The Sacramental Life

freedom will have an effect on our daily lives. Hope gives us the power to reach out in love to create new bonds of fellowship. Hope reminds us that we all have a place in God's Kingdom, so our communion with others is not dependent upon the particular persons we encounter. Hope challenges us to create possibilities for greater unity in the present as we await the final community of man with man.

Like faith and hope, love is a way of life based on our relationship with Christ. It is not a sentimental feeling we have now and then. Love is always creative because it is the power of Being itself. St. John was fond of reminding Christians that our God is Love. In the sacraments, Christ reaches out to us in love. He summons forth a creativity we did not know we had. He reveals possibilities for existing in ways we may have forgotten. He enriches our present by holding out to us a future without bounds. His Spirit empowers us to love as he loves.

Each sacramental meeting with Christ is an experience of a new dimension of love. This is more easily seen when we view love as a letting-be, in the sense of enabling another to be or to become. In love, Christ speaks to us about ourselves and discloses to us our potentialities for being. He shows us the capacity and power that we might never have come to know had he not revealed them to us. In love, we are called to share in Being and Being's concern for all that is. We are called to be and let-be. The love Christ offers to us is not measured according to our merits. He renews his offer of love even when we have not been responsive in the past. He wishes to share with us his own power to cherish others for their own sake, regardless of the return on our investment.

Someone once remarked: "The greatest gift we

can give to another is himself." That is what Christ's love is all about. His own life was an effort to help others discover their true selves. He continues in the sacraments to show us our potentialities for being, while empowering us to realize them. As Christians, we maintain our contact and association with Christ because we know that he alone can help us to realize what there is in us to be. We know that he is "the way, the truth, and the life."

What Christ discloses to us about ourselves can easily be hidden under a bushel basket. It can get lost or be swept away by the rush of events in our everyday lives. We can forget love's revelation. Then we are like the man, mentioned by St. Paul, who looked at himself in a mirror and then promptly forgot his appearance when he walked away. It is important that in each sacramental encounter we be disposed to let Christ transform us. He will not force us to respond. His love is not overpowering. His presence will not always be felt in great waves of emotion. Sometimes it may happen that, like Elijah, we hear the voice of the Lord not in the thunder and the storm, but in the gentle whisper of the breeze.

If the meeting with Christ in the sacraments is to be considered a religious experience, some knowledge of religious experience in general should promote our understanding of the sacraments. Every religious experience is an encounter with Holy Being; it is a meeting with a Sacred Other. In this experience, the Sacred reveals itself, but it also shows the believer who he is. In the encounter with Holy Being, the believer becomes aware of himself in a new way. He begins to see how he is related to the Holy, to himself, and to the world. He

The Sacramental Life

is enabled to transcend his previous limits in a new awareness of human existence.

In every real meeting with Christ, our sense of relatedness to the Father and to all of creation is strengthened. Christ shows us how events in our lives are inter-related and how they fit into God's creative design. Because sacraments are a means to achieving holiness or wholeness, they make us aware of "involvements," bonds of relatedness. The experience of Christ does not change the nature of our true involvements in the world of being, but it makes us more aware of how they all fit together. The awareness of the total picture liberates us. We become free only to the extent that we are aware of the world and where we stand in that world.

Even when we are not aware of it, the world of reality affects us. The value of the awareness awakened in a religious experience is that it lifts us above the natural course of events and helps us evaluate them in a new light. The type of self we become is related to the kind of awareness we reach. We can see this in the life of Christ, who was intensely aware of his relatedness to the Father, to himself, and to all created beings. In the sacraments, Jesus comes to free us. He comes to teach us the truth about ourselves and the world in which we live. We have to arouse ourselves so that we are not asleep when he comes to us. Of those who refused to come to a new awareness of reality, Jesus said: "They have eyes but see not; they have ears but hear not."

While there remain many things that might be said about sacraments, the dimensions considered in this chapter are not usually included in instruction on the sacraments. Yet, the theological virtues of faith, hope, and love are fundamental to the mature practice of one's religion. Placing them in the context of the kingdom promotes continuity in our understanding of sacraments. The Kingdom of God is the goal toward which all the sacraments are directed. The idea of the ultimate community of God and man helps us to avoid a narrow, individualistic interpretation of the sacraments.

DOCUMENTATION

The mystery of Christ is continued in the Church which is itself a sign of God's union with man. In the community of faith, Christ bestows his Spirit on the faithful through specific actions called sacraments. In the sacraments, it is Christ who acts to save us; the priest serves as his minister in the sacramental action. Sacraments are not just remedies for sin and its consequences. These sacramental encounters with Christ are sources of grace for both the individual and the community. As long as individuals grow in faith, the community will be a sign of Christ's presence in the world. (GCD 28, 55; RE/BT 10)

Of themselves, the sacraments express the will of Christ, but their full meaning cannot be understood apart from faith. Christ who offers us God's love and mercy in the sacraments needs our response if he is to touch us. It is important to cultivate the attitude of faith appropriate to each sacrament. When we respond, we allow the Holy Spirit to strengthen our freedom and enable us to live integrated lives. Integral personal growth, even growth in grace and the spiritual life, is not possible without community. It is especially in the Eucharist that Christian fellowship is fostered. Educa-

The Sacramental Life

tion has as its crucial task the understanding of the communal dimension of the sacraments. (GCD 56, 61; TT 24)

The sacraments have a threefold purpose: to make men holy, to build up the community of faith, and to worship the Triune God. These seven instruments of grace, because they are visible signs, are a means of education for the faithful. The very act of celebrating them helps to dispose our hearts to receive God's grace in a more fruitful manner. They encourage us to worship God daily and to care about our neighbor. If the sacraments are to instruct us, we must understand the signs. That is why religious education must include an interpretation of the sacramental ritual and the meaning of grace. The goal of such education must be lifelong sacramental living. (RE/BT 10)

Baptism establishes a permanent relationship between the individual and God. It is the sign of initiation into the faith community. Through this action of Christ, the believer is freed from both original and personal sin and raised to a new level of existence. Confirmation is linked to the sacrament of initiation. It is the sign of a mature Christian life, a sign of one's acceptance of the responsibility to carry the message of the Gospel to the world in which one lives. Two aspects of Penance must be balanced: pardon from God and reconciliation with the Church. Education in the sacrament of Penance must include adequate explanations of the concepts of forgiveness, confession, sorrow, and conversion. (GCD 57; RE/BT 11)

The Eucharist is the sacred meal which recalls the Last Supper. During this meal, we celebrate our unity in Christ and anticipate the banquet of the Kingdom of God. If we are truly celebrating, we must become more closely united with each other. Unless we make an attempt to rid ourselves of those things that separate us and destroy brotherhood, our worship is sterile. To feed on the Bread of Life is to care about all life and to be active in promoting the growth of that life. (RE/BT 11)

PART FOUR

SERVICE

We generally conceive of service in terms of doing; rarely do we think of service as being. What we can do is a consequence of who we are. In the Old Testament, God performed marvelous deeds so that the Israelites might learn who he is. The power of God could work miracles through Jesus of Nazareth because of who Jesus was. Jesus told his disciples they would be able to do great things provided they allowed themselves to be the persons they were called to be. So it seems that one of the greatest services Christians can render as individuals and as a community is to be who they say they are. Only those with a strong self-identity have the courage to allow others to be who they are.

10. The Moral Life

We often hear it said that Christians are no better than anybody else. Generally, the "better" is used in reference to the moral conduct of Christians. The evaluator in this case has deduced that the behavior of Christians is neither more human nor more humane than that of non-Christians. Historically, the conduct of Christians in general has not been morally superior to that of the rest of mankind. Furthermore, theologians remind us that our Christian identity cannot be defined in terms of our behavior. We know that membership in a community of faith does not eradicate moral problems. In the light of these observations, we might very well ask whether there really is such a thing as a Christian morality.

Christians themselves often confuse morality with religion, goodness with belief. To be a Christian is to be a good person. To be good, in turn, may mean: keeping the Ten Commandments of God, obeying the precepts of the Church, loving God and neighbor, doing good to others. None of these positions is exclusively Christian. Even the two great commands of Jesus are not the sole property of Christians. Does faith, then, make any difference in the way we relate to others? If we define morality merely in terms of publicly observable behavior or compliance with external regulations, Christians probably would not appear to be significantly different from others. Nor does the Gospel of Christ always demand that we be overtly different.

Both believers and non-believers are in general agreement that norms of morality are indispensable in any social group. But how they interpret those norms depends on their view of human existence, its nature and purpose. It is naive to claim that it does not matter what you believe as long as you are a decent human being. Morality must conform to the truth about human existence. In the light of his knowledge of the human condition, the moral philosopher tries to discover by reason how men ought to act. The moral theologian brings to his reflection the message of revelation to serve as a source for moral norms. It is the business of ethics to formulate general principles to guide human conduct. Human acts for which we are freely responsible and over which we have some rational control are said to be moral acts.

Morality is not a burden imposed on us from the outside. There can be no personal fulfillment or genuine happiness apart from the moral life. How we perceive our happiness will, of course, direct our pursuit of the good. Discerning the good is a matter involving heart and head, reason and emotions. On the level of feelings and sensibilities, the good is what is congenial, satisfying, healing, pleasant. We cannot separate feelings and desires from the good since, without them, we could not even be aware of anything good. But the problem with feelings is that they are not always reliable. The heart can lead us in many directions at once. Destructive choices can be made by people who are all heart. Our hearts yearn for all sorts of things which appear desirable yet lead to greater unrest and dissatisfaction. The problem comes not in having these feelings and desires, but in learning how to integrate them in our quest for wholeness.

We cannot maintain our personal integrity unless there is some rational consistency in the deliberate choices that we make. Integrity signifies wholeness or lack of division within oneself. It is a unity of mind and heart that comes when we bring our discordant impulses in line with our aspirations. This balance is not achieved by wishful thinking. Our lives become integrated wholes only when our decisions and moral choices are repeatedly aimed in the same direction. Psychologists tell us that personal commitment to an ideal or to a cause greater than ourselves gives us the power to unify our decisions and sort out our desires.

If our desires are not to cause division within us, we have to bring to them the light of reason. The heat of action can easily distract us from everything except the immediate good. Intelligent reflection on our own behavior can bring to our emotional state a purifying criticism. We can judge our own intentions. We can examine our aims in the light of our deeper commitment. Reflection helps us to see that what counts is not the intensity of a particular good, but the meaning it has for our total being. If we are to mature, we must set up a hierarchy of values on the basis of their importance in helping us reach our ultimate goal.

We can see, then, that external actions, while they are an important part of one's moral life, do not constitute the whole of morality. When we focus on particular acts and classify them as good or bad actions, our attention is concentrated on something outside the person. Jesus himself pointed out that sinful actions issue from a heart that is already disposed to do evil. If good trees bear good fruit and bad trees bear bad fruit, the condition of the fruit is a sign of the wholesomeness or sickness of the tree. This is indicative of the deeper dimension of morality.

Our understanding of the moral life will be no more profound than our understanding of the concepts of sin and freedom. The fundamental sin, as mentioned previously, is the failure to be who we are. It means stopping along the way and settling for a less meaningful existence. It is like Esau's selling his inheritance for a "mess of pottage." But awareness of a failure to be presupposes that we have some knowledge of our calling as human beings. It implies that we have subscribed to a particular view of human existence and our ultimate destiny as persons. It assumes that we have a clear idea of the direction we want our lives to take.

Without this direction, there can be no freedom. As pointed out in preceding chapters, freedom is not merely lack of restraint. It is not simply the power to do this or that specific act. It is the capacity to grow in humanness. It is the capacity to orient ourselves in a certain direction and to commit ourselves to our own ultimate wholeness and happiness. Our freedom is never complete. We always have the capacity to be more than we are. We can always enrich the meaning of our lives and gain a more comprehensive picture of where we are and where we would like to be.

The aspect of morality that is related to these dimensions of sin and freedom is what some theologians call our fundamental option. It is our most basic moral decision, our decision to be. It is a freely chosen attitude toward the ultimate good of human life. This choice lies at the very core of our being. Because it is so deeply rooted in our being, it gives meaning to everything else that we do. It underlies all other choices.

The Moral Life

There is continual resonance between this option and the particular acts that we choose to do. When our actions are congruent with our fundamental option, we deepen our commitment and give our daily activity a more profound unity and meaning. When we act against it, we introduce division within ourselves. A guilty conscience is a sign that we have acted against our own decision about who we are and can be.

It is at this fundamental level of moral decision that morality can be distinctively Christian. St. Paul said it well: "For me, to live is Christ." In other words, Jesus is not merely the exemplar of ethical conduct. To live as a Christian means to grow in Christhood. To be Christ is to assume his attitude toward all life. It means accepting his vision of the Father's plan for our own happiness. To be Christ is to direct all our activity toward the Father and to seek God's Kingdom above everything else. The Scriptures tell us: "Have this mind in you which was also in Christ Jesus. . . ." But the decision to assume the mental outlook of Christ does not mean that we will not fail. It does not mean that each moral act that we perform will be compatible with that outlook.

We know from our own experience that irrational elements take over now and then. Often, immediate gratification seems more satisfying than the unity and wholeness of our personhood. This is where the idea of venial and mortal sins comes in. Venial sin is not more positive than mortal sin, but it occurs on a superficial level. It does not attack the core of our being. This does not mean that venial sin is not destructive. Each time we go against our fundamental option, we undermine its stability. The danger is that superficial failings can become habitual. When this happens, we can more easily forget Being. The Christian vision can become blurred. We can lose sight of who we are. Christ warned: "The little you have will be taken away."

We were often reminded in the past that a habit of venial sin could lead to serious sin. Such a process is analogous to the manner in which a married couple heads toward divorce. No divorce occurs overnight. One infraction does not cause a complete break. Usually in such a marriage there is a series of small hurts which are never healed. A growing number of offenses are never reconciled on a deep personal level. When this happens, the partners begin to look elsewhere for happiness. Habitual venial sin is like the series of infractions that can lead to a complete break in what had originally been an intimate personal relationship. Mortal sin is the divorce between creature and Creator. Man is no longer interested in being God's partner in creation. That is why, in Christian tradition, mortal sin has always been considered deadly. Such sin is a refusal to live life in the light of Being; it prefers to walk alone in darkness.

Whether we decide to walk in light or darkness, our choice helps to determine the moral principles that will guide our conduct. We do not always bring to consciousness the principles on which we are acting. We need to reflect upon our moral acts in order to find out what we are affirming by our behavior. We may be saying one thing and doing another. A moral principle is not something we gather merely from the facts of the situation. It is a rule of action that we have freely adopted. To hold a moral principle is to subscribe personally to a particular view about the way things ought to be. The moral principle is justified not by my intention but by the consequences of putting it into practice.

The Moral Life

The principle is to be judged by its effects. Jesus remarked: "By their fruits you will know them."

Moral principles are themselves matters of choice and decision. It is not the case that we can act with or without principles. Any genuine choice of alternatives involves, at least implicitly, the adoption of a principle of conduct. Every real choice makes actual one set of possibilities in preference to another. The position that we adopt says that we are committed to one particular view of human life rather than another. Our decision is a practical declaration of the way things ought to be. Either we choose the principles by which our lives are guided or we allow somebody else to do the choosing for us. "Not to decide is to decide" (H. Cox). If we want to be free, we must have the courage to be who we say we are. Authentic personhood demands fidelity to the call of Being.

Fidelity, like freedom, is earned; it is not given to us as a gift just waiting to be unwrapped. Fortunately, we have the power to detect when we are being deflected away from our primary commitment. We can sense when we are "falling away from the faith." The power by which we sense that we are or have been unfaithful is our conscience. Conscience is the awareness of how well we are succeeding or how far we are failing to make actual our potentialities for being. It is the self's own awareness of how it measures up to itself. Conscience indicates the measure of agreement between our conduct and our value-system.

Conscience is not a product of Christian tradition, but the person and word of Christ are the standards against which the Christian measures himself. The saving work of Christ lights up our existence and raises it to a new level of meaning. But grace is always accompanied by judgment. As soon as we are enabled to see the greatness of our calling, we begin to realize how far we still have to go. Our natural awareness of sin is heightened and intensified by the Spirit. We begin to notice our failures in a new way and to understand the nature of sin more profoundly. To be aware of sin is to be dissatisfied with ourselves. In our awareness, we are already seeking to turn away from where we are. This is what is meant by repentance. When we repent, we turn ourselves around to seek once more the way of salvation. We would not be able to take even the first step in the right direction if God did not take the initiative. "No one can come to me unless the Father who sent me draws him."

It is because of sin and the fact that we turn away from the good that we need laws, a morality of obligation. A self-giving love that goes beyond the law is the ideal. Until we all arrive at that level, we shall continue to need laws. The Church remains a community of sinners. Those who are strong must support the weaker members. But the strong are not perfect. As long as we are subject to the human condition, our moral choices will be tinged with ambiguity. Even the most dedicated person is capable of confusing his own self-interest with the cause of God. At every stage of moral development, we can use the collective wisdom of the Church, which has found, through the centuries, that certain kinds of behavior have destructive consequences.

While it is true that laws can become hardened and distorted, they are intended to protect the way of life that the Church proclaims. They are meant to promote growth in holiness. The rules always tell us something about the implications of our moral choices. No community can preserve its values or its identity without at least some minimum standards for its members. But the law is never perfect. There must be room for ethical creativity in new situations. This does not mean that we ought to be allowed to set aside the rules from one situation to another. When we find that the rules do not promote growth in Christ, the community should be encouraged to reexamine its position. We can trust that the Spirit is still guiding the Church.

When we reflect on the Church laws that affect our everyday lives, we find that only infrequently are we commanded to contribute something positive to the realization of the good. Most of the time, the laws merely provide minimal standards of conduct. Sometimes the laws are stated as prohibitions. These are designed to keep us from wandering too far from center. Sometimes, people get the impression that the Church obliges us over and beyond the demands of the Gospel. Actually, it is the other way around. The law merely gets us started on the way to a life lived according to the Gospel. The self-giving love of Christ is much more difficult to live up to than any ecclesiastical regulation.

In the matter of law, it is easy to go to extremes. The legalist places his hope in his observance of the law. He feels secure when he has not broken any rules. The rules insure salvation. Such legalism is unchristian. Jesus made it clear that "The Sabbath was made for man, not man for the Sabbath." Rules must serve people and promote justice. We have to bring to our observance of the law the power of reason tempered by love. Many times, St. Paul had to remind his converts that the law has no power to save. Paul made it clear that Christians place their trust not in the law but in Christ.

At the other extreme, we find the situationist. He claims that rules are irrelevant because each situation is unique. Each situation must be judged on its own merits. It is not related to other situations in which we might find ourselves. The situationist says that acting from habit is mechanical, not human. The only human response to a situation is, to him, the spontaneous one. Such a position makes of our lives a series of unconnected acts. Yet we know that moral decisions can never be limited to meeting the demands of a particular situation. Our decisions are affected by our personal history. The decisions we made in the past limit and qualify our power to act rightly in the present. Our present moral choices inevitably affect our future capacity to make the right decisions. Good habits may protect us from our own weakness in a particular situation and strengthen our capacity to make a right decision. The kind of persons we have been and shall be is involved in every moral decision.

The situationist goes further. He suggests that the only rule in any situation is the rule of love. It certainly is true that the Christian moral life must be founded on love. But merely knowing that we ought to love does not resolve the difficulty in moral decisions. In any particular situation the Christian, like anybody else, may have to consider a multiplicity of elements. Rarely is our decision a clear-cut decision between good and evil. Many times, we have to choose between things, each of which has some value and some potential perversity. Sometimes either alternative seems desirable or defensible. Not everyone has arrived at such a high level of maturity that he can easily discern the most loving thing to do. Even the most enlightened may have to call on the resources of the Christian community for guidance.

The Christian's relation to the law must be interpreted in terms of Christ. Our identity as Christians is tied to our faith in Christ and the degree to which its meaningfulness permeates our lives. As Christians, we are shaped in our dispositions and intentions by the faith of the Christian community. In this community, Christ is the norm for our moral purposes even when some other norm would be more convenient or expedient at a particular point in time. If Christ is the norm, all that he stands for and symbolizes has authority for us. As we strengthen our relationship with Christ, our love is stabilized. As we become more intimately united with Christ, he commands us from within rather than from the outside.

All this raises the question of its practical application in the classroom. We know that conscience is not furnished at birth, although the capacity for conscience may be present. One is not born with ideas of what is right and what is wrong. Parents and teachers use rewards and punishments, repetitions and emphasis in helping the child to learn the difference. A child cannot be expected to know why he must perform some acts and avoid others. He cannot understand reasons for approval or disapproval. Praise and blame are purely external.

On the sensual level, the child interprets events according to the pleasure or pain they afford him. So he begins to associate badness with punishment. He avoids certain acts, not because he sees that the act is wrong, but because he knows that pain will follow. Sin is a purely religious concept and cannot be grasped at this level. Adults who were taught at a very young age that every little bad action was a sin learned to associate God's punishment with particular acts. Anyone who has had this experience knows how long this notion lingers in the mind. Such a notion not only inhibits growth in morality but also distorts the Christian concept of God. The child learns to fear God for the wrong reasons.

There is nothing in pedagogy that prohibits our appealing to the child's desire to be good. Young children like to be thought of as good little boys and girls. Commending appropriate behavior and showing how such behavior makes everybody happy can motivate the children to do their best. It is not healthy to motivate them by instilling an irrational fear of the punishments of God. This does not imply that reward and punishment have no place in the training of the young. Growth comes through conflict and challenge as well as acceptance. But the child should not be given the impression that God is going to "get even" with him for each little fault and failing.

Like any other component of the personality, the conscience must keep pace with the individual's growth toward maturity. Conscience is always a present guide to conduct. It helps an individual relate to reality as he conceives it at the time. Children on the objective level interpret the good largely in terms of rules laid down by adults. They do not yet have an interiorized set of values. Because their self-identity is not yet firmly rooted, they need leadership and external authority to guide their conduct. If they have learned to trust adults, they will accept some adult values. Through such trust, they can be helped to develop at least an elementary system of personal values.

A personal value system is a prerequisite for a responsible conscience. During early adolescence, the student may go through a period of naive negativism, demanding proofs and reasons for everything. He may be extremely rationalistic. He understands concrete sins but not the concept of the fundamental sin. Since he can deal with actual sins, he should be given the opportunity to explicitate his reasons for judging specific acts to be sinful or commendable. This helps him clarify his own ideas about morality. The teacher who insists on doing all his reasoning for him does not help him grow.

On the other hand, the student must be guided to see dimensions of reality that he overlooks in his reasoning about morals. For the sake of peace and harmony in the classroom, the teacher may be tempted to go along with him and agree with all that he says. If the teacher avoids challenging him and demands nothing, the student may develop what is sometimes called a neurosis of meaning. If there is no right or wrong, anything goes. Since there is no need to make personal decisions, life loses its meaning. As one student said of her mother: "I wish she would say yes or no, but all she says is, 'If that's what you want, dear.' "

Once a student has developed a personal value system and has an idea of the religious commitment he wishes to make, he should be able to grasp the notion of the fundamental option, along with the deeper dimensions of freedom and sin. On the spiritual level, he should be challenged by a more profound understanding of morality and of what it means in terms of his Christian identity. Since students at this level are generally disillusioned with external authority, they can be helped to discover their own authority as self-directed persons. They need to know that there is more to Christian morality than compliance with law, but they should not get the idea that going beyond the law means fewer responsibilities. When we allow Christ to rule us from within, the demands we place upon ourselves are greater than the obligations of external law.

Some of the problems among Catholic adults today stem from their identification of law with morality. Civil law, which sets minimum standards, never the ideal, becomes the norm guiding our conduct. If the law says something is allowed, it is accepted, even though it falls far below Christian standards. If the law states that we can now abort a fetus, it must be all right to do so. It is not very helpful to say that abortion is wrong because the Church is against it. This does not help us to understand why it is wrong. Very few adults speak of sin as a reversal of the creative process of letting-be. Rarely do they ask which moral decision will help them grow in humanness, in genuine care and concern for others. Seldom do they inquire about which alternative promotes the unity of being. Most of the time, they dispute civil law by appealing to Church law. But the meaning of life is not dependent upon law.

Obviously, the appetite for meaning differs from person to person. Some are satisfied sooner than others. Not everyone has the same capacity for contemplation or comprehension. It may be that some have neither the ability nor the inclination to make use of deeper symbols or theory. Nevertheless, students have a right to know that there is a dimension of meaning that can have a profound effect on the way they view their relations with others. On this level, values take on a more generalized and symbolic character. That is why adults at this level are not overly concerned with immediate satisfaction. Their joy and satisfaction come not only from fulfillment, but also from the knowledge that they are committed to that which can bring ultimate satisfaction. In fact, just holding the values keeps them moving toward the goal.

The Moral Life

Students ought to be helped to progress to a more creative and enriching level of existence. Helping them to do so is analogous to starting a chemical reaction. Electrons that move around the nucleus of an atom are content to remain at the lowest energy levels. As they move round and round in their own orbital shells, nothing happens. But as soon as a stimulus is applied which gets the electrons seeking higher energy levels, the atom can reach out, so to speak, to form a bond with another atom. The result of this creativity is a new compound unlike either element in its constitution.

Morality, then, is not simply a matter of learning the rules. It is a matter of learning how to respond more and more freely to the call of Being. It means learning who we are and what we are called to be. It involves commitment to a personal set of values which grow more symbolic as we mature. These values which take us beyond ourselves are capable not only of satisfying us, but also of expanding our horizons. They can broaden the character of our religious faith and permeate our lives at a profound level.

DOCUMENTATION

Christian morality is our response to God who invites us to a life of intimacy with him. Christian morality outlines a way of living that is consonant with the dignity of one who wishes to live as a child of God. Jesus showed us by his own life how to live in obedience to a loving Father. He sent us the Spirit to enable us, with his gifts, to live this new life. (RE/BT 17)

The special characteristic of the Christian moral life is its total relationship to the love of God. The faith that we profess leads us to give expression to our commitment in signs of love. Just as Christ reached out to unite men in love, so the Christian moves out to others. The follower of Christ knows that he grows in the image of God as he reaches out to form bonds of unity and love. He sees this life of love as his greatest responsibility and as the source of his highest dignity. (RE/BT 18)

The Christian has toward God the attitude of a son to an all-loving Father. Uppermost in his mind and in his scale of values is the will of the Father. The true Christian is so aware of his relationship with God that he can never think or live as if he were independent of his Creator. What he believes has a marked effect on what he does or avoids. His faith enables him to respond generously to the demands of love. (RE/BT 18)

Only in freedom can man direct himself toward goodness. Freedom itself is a sign of the divine image in man. Man's dignity demands that he act according to a knowing and free choice. Such a choice is personally motivated and prompted from within. Man achieves such dignity when he pursues his ultimate goal in his personal choice of what is good. He grows in freedom as he learns to procure for himself those means that will help him arrive at his final goal. (GS 17)

Freedom needs to be guided through the problems that arise in day-to-day living. An informed conscience can help us achieve a higher level of freedom. Conscience is a personal judgment that something is right or wrong in the light of our understanding of God's will for us. If we are to be at peace with ourselves, we must follow our conscience. The teaching authority of the Church gives guidance in applying enduring norms and values to specific situations. As Catholic Christians, we

The Moral Life

pay respectful attention to the standards of morality laid down by the Church. These can prevent us from harming ourselves through our own shortsightedness. The more a correct conscience holds sway, the more we turn aside from blind choice and strive to be guided by objective norms that have been proven to produce good fruit. (RE/BT 17; GS 16)

11. The Kingdom and the Future

Day after day, Christians pray "Thy kingdom come." The whole ministry of Jesus was a proclamation of the kingdom. Christ exhorted his followers to seek the kingdom above everything else. The kingdom is to have top priority in the Christian's set of values. Being a Christian, then, implies dedication to the kingdom and its future fulfillment. Yet, if we were to ask Christians what the kingdom means in their lives and how it affects their decisions, they would probably admit that, for the most part, they are hardly aware of it.

The problem with the notion of the kingdom does not lie in the indifference of Christians. Many Christians are not aware of the connotations of the phrase, Kingdom of God. To contemporary Americans kingdoms are an archaism. Most people are not attracted by the symbol of a kingdom. Theologians emphasize our responsibility to change our shared symbols when these no longer convey divine reality. Sometimes, we have to use different images to get across the idea of the biblical symbol. That is why many people prefer to speak of God's Kingdom as the power of the future. One reason for this change is that the dynamism of the future brings into proper focus the theology of hope.

Hope is at the heart of human existence. It seeks

to express itself at every level of human life. Without hope, we grow listless, dull, or apathetic. When we are deprived of hope, we lose our freedom to go beyond the present moment into the future. We succumb to the finality of the present condition. To be free is to have a future. To be free is to be able to transcend the present situation. Without such freedom, hope is meaningless. When we are free, we can stand before our possibilities and take the action needed to actualize them. Hope in a real future gives us the power to change the present. Hope looks to the future while acting in the present.

The present is not just a moment on the way to becoming. It is not just an infinitesimal dot on an infinite time line. Now is the moment when we stand before our Creator and answer yes or no to Being. We face our future now. But facing the future is not simply being related to it. Facing the future means participating in its creation in freedom and hope. We do this by creating an atmosphere that is conducive to growth in being. We increase the unity of human existence by forming bonds of conscious relatedness to others in the light of our common future.

The unity of all things is continuous with creation. God confers being, he sustains it, and he intends to bring it to completion. The unity of being that is broken by our self-centeredness must be made whole. This unity is achieved through reconciliation. Reconciliation is the activity whereby the disorders of existence are straightened out, the estrangements healed, the contradictions resolved. This reconciliation process was begun by Jesus in his inauguration of the kingdom: ". . . the valleys shall be filled; the crooked ways made straight."

This reconciliation process will find its completion in God's Kingdom. The unity of creation will be realized when God's promise is fulfilled. In the Scriptures, Yahweh promises his people a land and a savior. Jesus promises his Spirit; he promises to come again; he promises a new heaven and a new earth. So to live by hope is to live by God's promises. As Christians, we wait for God. We wait for the God who is also the fulfillment of his promises. But we are always tempted to dwell in a comfortable, secure present as though the moment of fulfillment had arrived. To fix our gaze only on the present would be to dissolve our hope. Not even a transfiguration is the ultimate fulfillment of the kingdom. Peter's suggestion about pitching three tents on Mount Tabor went unheeded. Instead, the apostles were commanded to place their immediate experience in the context of a future resurrection event.

That resurrection event is also the future of all mankind. Through faith in Jesus, Christians are already certain of a future participation in the resurrection life. The full reality of God's Kingdom on earth will be realized only in the future life of resurrection. We can orient ourselves toward the kingdom now by living the life of communion with others that we will live then. We can begin to show in our lives some of the qualities of that ultimate community of men united in God's love. We can begin to accept human situations not as they are, but as they can be. We can begin to judge human events in the light of our common future, the kingdom.

The kingdom is not something apart from God; otherwise, we would have no business seeking it first. God and his kingdom are inseparable. His kingdom will not be established by man. It is not something that is reached as an outgrowth of that which is already present. God's future is the arrival of something new.

The Kingdom and the Future

We anticipate the newness, we pray for it, we hope for it. To believe in Jesus is to keep our future open by allowing him to release its power into our present. Jesus made use of the power of the future in his own life. His message was new and refreshing. His deeds were signs of things to come.

Jesus' words will continue to be good news as long as Christians keep it alive with the newness of the future. The living Word brings the future of life so near that we can already taste it. The power of this future should motivate us to work for community among men. We cherish the vision of the kingdom even though we know that whatever we bring about is merely provisional. We know that we do not have the perfect blueprint for changing the present. But our satisfaction does not come from the perfection of what we have accomplished, but in the glory of the end toward which we are moving. We are inspired to work for peace and justice among men until the King comes to make all things new.

Among the ancients, the king was the mediator between God and man. It was his function to destroy the enemies of the kingdom and to establish true justice. Because of his wise government, the members of the kingdom would experience peace and joy. So the Kingdom of God refers to that perfect society which will replace the temple and the church. The Book of Revelation tells us: ". . . the temple will be no more." In this kingdom, everyone will know the will of God and respond to it. We will be united in Being and with each other in a love that allows each person to be who he is. Because the light of Being will shine through all, the holiness of God will be fully manifested. God will be all in all.

Our hope in this future is not some kind of naive optimism. Christian hope takes seriously the fact of sin and evil. It is because of sin and its effects that we hope for deliverance. We do not hope unless we perceive that something is lacking or something is wrong. When we are in distress, we are not hopeful unless we anticipate the possibility of being rescued. If we are in darkness, we long for the break of day. "There's got to be a morning after!" Hope says that our present tribulation is not the end of the trail. Hope does not deny the unpleasant facts by pretending all is well when, in fact, man is in misery. But hope refuses to accept present injustices as the final judgment about how things must be. Hope takes evil seriously by anticipating the only power that can overcome all injustice.

The power that redresses all wrongs is the power of God's future. We know that man and his world are destined for Holy Being. We know they will find completion and fulfillment in God. The God who creates is also the destiny toward which all created beings are drawn. To believe in one God is to believe that his power dominates all. But power is meaningless without a future. God holds the future in his hands, so to speak. This future is the same for all of us. There is only one future and every man shares in it. The future we Christians hope for for ourselves must be the same future that we anticipate for all mankind.

The idea of unity of being and our sharing in the same future seems unfair when we measure ourselves by the number of deeds that we perform. Jesus told a parable about workers in the vineyard which is relevant here. Some of those who were hired worked long hours for the owner of the vineyard; those who came later in the day worked only a short time. Yet, all the workers

The Kingdom and the Future 167

were invited to share in the same future. Those workers who focused their attention on their own activity complained that, in the eyes of the vineyard owner, all the workers were equal. When Christians think that being a chosen people means that they are destined for special privileges apart from the rest of mankind, they are acting like the grumbling workers in the vineyard. As Christians, we have our special privileges now. We know the owner of the vineyard and experience his presence in a special way. Through our present relationship with him, we are getting a foretaste of things to come.

Even though the same future awaits everyone, not everyone is aware of it. The Church is the community of those who are conscious of their future. The Church makes explicit its anticipation of the kingdom. Christians know that Jesus himself promised to go ahead of them and prepare a place for them. What the Church already enjoys is a foretaste of what the world still has in store for it. But the Church itself is not the kingdom. The very notion of church presupposes a wider community which it serves.

Within this larger society, the Church plays an indispensable role. Every religious community attempts to locate human existence within a context of a meaningful whole. The Church contributes to the personal integration of human existence by confronting man with the ultimate mystery of life. The Church promotes the unity of mankind by making known God's purposes in history. In this awareness, we are given a sense of priorities. The final goal of humanity gives meaning to all our activity and provides an absolute standard for evaluating all our works.

One thing this standard makes apparent is that no

political form of society provides ultimate human satisfaction either for individuals or groups. No form of human life is exclusively and absolutely the fulfillment of humanity. As Karl Rahner puts it: "No community is ever the final configuration of human destiny." That is why the Church must play a critical role in society. The Church exposes the limitations of all present forms of social and political life. It does this by confronting man with the reality of his own glorious destiny. The Church encourages hope by reminding us that things can be better.

The Church cannot carry out its mission of hope unless the vision of the kingdom is at the center of its message. It must show that the Gospel is interested in the world's tomorrow. When the Church no longer inspires hope, it becomes superfluous. There is no way of serving God without serving the world. It is not God who needs our service, but the world of mankind for whom Christ died. This world is on the way to a future goal. To reach that goal, it must be changed until, by the transforming power of God's future, it is brought to completion. It is the function of the Church to inhibit the manufacture of idols along the way to the future. When we allow anything to block the path of hope, cloud the vision, or give us a false sense of security in the present, we have built an idol. It is the golden calf around which we dance when we should be on our way to the land that God promises.

The Church is always in tension with any manner of thinking that accepts the world as it is. In fact, the community of faith can never be satisfied with the Church as it is either. Both Church and world must continually reform. The Church must be a progressive force for human dignity in the wider society. If it is to practice what it preaches, the Church must examine its own structures in order to determine whether or not they promote unity of being. Participation in the kingdom frees us from every other ultimate authority. We are free to judge everything in its light. There are no privileged areas exempt from critical reflection.

When we think that everything in the Church is as it should be, we forget the preliminary character of all forms of human life. It is a perversion to think of the future as a prolongation of what is already existing. When we are set in our ways, we close ourselves to the future and its promise of change. When individuals or communities assert themselves against the future, they miss their authentic existence. They are unfaithful to the call to exist in full openness toward what is to be. They give up their participation in the ongoing work of creation which always brings new life.

Wherever man responds to God's revelation, he is inevitably directed toward community with others. We expect this to happen in the Church, but God's activity is not confined to the Church. The Kingdom of God triumphs whenever men create conditions of equality, justice, and freedom. All human justice participates in some way in God's justice. But God's justice is not established anywhere in its final form. No social order of justice is capable of realizing full community of brotherhood. Every form of human justice remains provisional.

Just because no form of justice is perfect, it does not follow that our efforts are meaningless. The vision of the future is what gives meaning to our quest for justice, peace, and love. Since the kingdom is inseparably connected with our destiny, we cannot give up the goal of a perfect community among men. We know that love is the final norm of justice. At the heart of love is the concern for the possibilities that exist for the other person. We respect the other as a person when we know that the same infinite destiny that is at work in ourselves is at work in him. We are truly just when we care enough about that person that we want him to realize his possibilities.

The love that is at work in the development of greater justice does not deliver us from sin. Because of sin, there can be no perfect community. Individuals and groups use social arrangements for their own gain. They cut themselves off from common tasks. The compulsion of the law remains unavoidable. Laws are subordinate to justice and must serve justice. But even just laws do not free us from the dividedness of human existence brought about by greed and selfishness.

Christians are too realistic to ignore the existence of sin and its destructive consequences. They do not seek through their human accomplishments to create a paradise on earth. But they stand in the midst of the struggle and dare to act according to principles of justice, peace, and reconciliation. They seek to bring the power of the future to bear on situations already poisoned by hate or vindictiveness. They seek solutions that acknowledge the dignity of the human person. They seek to establish structures that serve man better. They try to change those things that block justice and to eradicate those that set men against men.

The Christian's efforts for peace and human dignity are informed by his vision of the integration of all human life in God. The Christian community must take seriously its function to proclaim the kingdom and prepare for it. The task of the Church has always been one of service. Even at its inception, the Church was char-

The Kingdom and the Future

acterized by brotherhood, love, and service. But this does not mean that the Church has to be a social action agency. The Church does not have the capacity to do all the social work for the world. That is not its mission. But the Church must set the world free to do its task. The Church can make society aware of its responsibilities in safeguarding all forms of human existence. It must promote those political structures that enhance human life. The Church must offer hope to all those who are beginning to wonder if there really is a way out of the enveloping darkness.

Recent studies in the psychology of hope provide insights which Christians might find helpful as they endeavor to improve social conditions. Psychologists found that the quality of the action taken by a person is relative to his hopefulness in a situation. When the goal has a high probability of being attained and the goal is important, the person working toward the goal experiences much joy, pleasure, and satisfaction. He does not attain the goal by himself. Other people are not merely relevant to hope, but their very actions determine the individual's potential for attaining the goal. His hopefulness is influenced by what others tell him about the goal. His perception that he is part of a unified group influences his level of hopefulness. Often, his security is a function of the power and the friendliness of other people in the situation.

It seems, then, that the importance we attach to the final goal of all humanity will have an effect on the way we conceive our service to the human community. If we are to release the power of the future to do its work in the present, we have to take seriously the sermon on the mount. The beatitudes provide a guide for the Christian conscience. By these words, Jesus instituted a moral revolution which is still far from completion. He disowns wealth and status as marks of human achievement. He repudiates even the power or influence a person may have achieved through aggressiveness or self-assertion. He praises the single-hearted, those who serve God loyally for his own sake and not for self-interest. He blesses those who work for reconciliation among men. Those who work for justice and peace will have the happiness of seeing their work completed in the kingdom.

Working for justice and peace is no simple task. When situations get tense, it is all too easy to react, instead of responding to the real issues. If we are to improve matters and not merely complicate them, we have to know what we are dealing with. We have to make an effort to understand how things really are, rather than merely dictate how they must be. We may have to come to grips with history and process. When violence erupts on an individual or communal level, it is usually a sign of a past history of frustration. A recent study of men and women in old-age homes showed that those who remained healthy and lived longer were quite aggressive. These individuals found that only by being assertive could they maintain some control over their own futures. Those old people who did not fight frustration lost hope and became listless. We can see, then, that simply condemning the aggressive does not improve the social conditions that foster hostility.

All this might make us wonder how it fits into religious education. Young children can understand that Jesus came to tell us about the wonderful world our Father has planned for us. In this world, we shall all be friends. There will be no crying because we shall not get hurt any more. There will be no spankings be-

The Kingdom and the Future

cause we shall be doing the right things. But we have to get ready now. We have to start now to be friends with everyone. We have to start now to do what is right for us to do. While children can readily understand these things, they will learn to hope only if they can trust adults. They will learn to hope in God's promises when they see that adults always keep their promises. Unfulfilled promises are disenchanting.

At the objective level, children are concerned with concrete justice that is realized now. They hope for particular things, rather than growth in being. The preparation for the future kingdom is a matter of doing those good deeds that are expected of them. Their good deeds are not aimed primarily at promoting community among men. They do not necessarily promote awareness of one's relatedness to others at a deeper level. But these students can learn something about the elementary forms of justice. They are interested in being fair with one another and in being treated fairly themselves. They can be led to examine their own practices in their peer groups to see how fair they are in their dealings with outsiders. While they are too young to do much to change the social conditions in which they find themselves, they can be made aware of ways in which unjust social conditions develop.

On the spiritual level, the power of God's future can be a motivating force in the life of the believer. Students at this level can understand that love is a matter of creating conditions that promote human possibilities. They can understand that much of what passes as "charity" is the bedfellow of injustice. Certain forms of charity merely impose on the recipient an obligation to be grateful to the donor, while the cause of his need is overlooked. While they know that we are not going to create the perfect community of justice and love, they can try to leave conditions a little better than they found them.

Christians do not have to wait for the Church to tell them what to do. They can be guided by their interests and talents to enter those areas where they can be effective in promoting human welfare. The vision of the kingdom can help to remind them that it is not a hopeless task. Students ought to realize that they are not going to change the world overnight, nor are they going to do it alone. Since they have to start somewhere, they might begin by examining their own situations and what they do in their private lives to foster recognition of the rights and dignity of others. They can examine their own consciences to see if they really do wish for others the same joy in the kingdom that they wish for themselves.

As Christians, then, we have hope because we know we have a future. We look to this future for the source of power to change the present. This power was evidenced in Jesus' life and resurrection. Christ brings into our lives the same power of resurrection. He frees us to become who we truly are. His kingdom is the hope of man in all ages. This hope impels Christians to pray: ". . . for yours is the kingdom and the power and the glory now and forever."

DOCUMENTATION

Christian hope is of special importance today as a middle-ground between two extremes. On the one hand, many people express naive optimism which fails to admit the reality and effects of sin upon individuals and

The Kingdom and the Future

society. At the other extreme, we find others who, because they are fully aware of evil in themselves and society, are tempted to despair. In the face of these two attitudes, the Church can make a unique contribution by preaching the gospel of hope. The gospel proclaims the dignity of man and the freedom of each person. It gives assurance that men are right to hope for salvation and the ultimate conquest of sin, injustice, privation, and death. It reminds us that these things have already been vanquished in the person of Christ. (TT 9)

A person who is mature in faith directs his thoughts and desires to the fulfillment of the kingdom. Religious education can help the believer grow in maturity by directing his hope to the goal of the future. It must make him aware of the fact that the notion of the kingdom demands his cooperation in the undertakings of the human race for improvements in human society. In fact, Pope Paul VI has stated that social needs must in the years to come have a dominant place in our preoccupations. (GCD 29)

It is the educational mission of the Church to see the dignity of human life with the vision of Jesus and to involve itself in the search for solutions to the pressing problems of society. Christians are obliged to seek justice and peace in the world. Catholics, both as individuals and as community, should join wherever possible with all persons of good will in an effort to solve social problems in ways that consistently reflect Gospel values. Special knowledge and skills are needed for the effective pursuit of justice and peace. Christian education, therefore, is basic to the effort to fulfill the demands of the Gospel and to discern the practical demands of justice. While the task is difficult, it cannot be dispensed with. (TT 10,11)

The future of humanity is in the hands of those who are strong enough to provide coming generations with reasons for living and hoping. Through hope, the Christian community is filled with the expectation of the kingdom. This vision enables them to think correctly about human and earthly goods by putting them into proper perspective. We must not minimize the responsibility everyone has regarding our future destiny. On the day of the Lord's coming, the entire Church will reach her perfection and enter into the fullness of God. This is the foundation of the hope and the prayer of the Christian who prays "thy kingdom come." (GS 31; GCD 44, 69)

Growth in Christ's Kingdom must be distinguished from mere earthly progress. Nevertheless, to the extent that progress fosters values of human dignity, brotherhood, and freedom, it is of vital concern to the Kingdom of God. The expectation of a new earth must not weaken, but rather stimulate, our concern for this present world. All that we do for the kingdom will be transfigured by Christ who will hand the kingdom over to his Father. He will transform it into a kingdom of "truth and life, holiness and grace, justice, love and peace." (GS 39)

The Church, a visible assembly and a spiritual community, goes forward with humanity and experiences the same earthly lot the world does. The Church serves as a leaven and as a kind of soul for society. The Church carries out her saving purpose by her impact on the dignity of the human person and by the way in which she strengthens the seams of human society. The community of faith inspires hope when it imbues the everyday activity of man with a deeper meaning and importance. (GS 40)

The Kingdom and the Future 177

Christ gave his Church no proper mission in the political, economic, or social order. The purpose of the Church is a religious one. However, out of this religious mission comes the light and energy which can serve to structure and unify the human community according to the will of God. When circumstances create the need, the Church can and must initiate activities on behalf of all men. This is particularly true of activities designed for the needy. While the Church supports all those social movements whose purposes are the enhancement of human life, it is not bound by any one political or social order. Universal in its scope, the Church works for the unity of all nations and peoples. (GS 42)